*M*USIC
for YOUR
HEART

ACE COLLINS

MUSIC *for* YOUR HEART

REFLECTIONS *from* YOUR FAVORITE SONGS

Abingdon Press
NASHVILLE

MUSIC FOR YOUR HEART
REFLECTIONS FROM YOUR FAVORITE SONGS

Copyright © 2013 by Ace Collins

Library of Congress Cataloging-in-Publication Data

Collins, Ace.
  Music for your heart : reflections from your favorite songs and hymns / Ace Collins.
       pages cm
  ISBN 978-1-4267-6727-2 (binding: soft-back / pbk. : alk. paper) 1. Popular music—Religious aspects. 2. Christian life. I. Title.
  ML3921.8.P67C63 2013
  781.64'112—dc23

                                                                                          2013011034

13 14 15 16 17 18 19 20 21 22—10 9 8 7 6 5 4 3 2 1

MANUFACTURED IN THE UNITED STATES OF AMERICA

*T*O ALL THE MEMBERS WHO
HAVE BEEN A PART OF
THE VARSITY DINER HOME GROUP!

Contents

Contents

Contents

Contents

*I*f You're Happy and You Know It

Although you've never seen him, you love him. Even though you don't see him now, you trust him and so rejoice with a glorious joy that is too much for words. —*1 Peter 1:8*

"If You're Happy and You Know It" is one of the first children's songs many kids learn in elementary school. The tune, which may have originated as a Latvian folk song, likely goes back almost two centuries. The melody is upbeat, incredibly catchy, and easy to learn. The song's lyrics, written in the first part of the twentieth century, were surely penned with children in mind. The repetitive words are a call to action requiring everything from the clapping of hands to the stomping of feet. To hear the tune almost always brings a smile, and when sung, "If You're Happy and You Know It" is a complete mood changer.

A recent poll found that a majority of young adults find Christians to be judgmental and unhappy. Being an unaccepting sourpuss is a great way to drive people away from anything. Few folks gravitate to someone whose face wears a frown or a scowl and who is always pointing fingers. Yet those who smile and laugh while parading through life with energy and expression usually lead a parade of people who want to catch what they have.

Countless times in the Scripture, we are told that believers are to be happy and worry-free. So why is that so hard for many in the church body to embrace? Perhaps it is because their hearts and minds are in the wrong place. They are dwelling on things they can't change rather than looking for ways to make an impact.

Dr. Albert Schweitzer chose to make an impact. He picked one of the toughest callings in the world. His life as a missionary in Africa was never easy. He had to win the trust of people who wondered if he was just like all the other Europeans who had exploited them in the past. Even when he cleared that hurdle, he lived without creature comforts for a half-century, spent years as a prisoner of war, had to rebuild his facilities several times, and had to make long treks through the jungle just to reach those he was trying to save. In spite of these hardships, Schweitzer always wore a huge smile on his face. When people asked how he could be so happy in the midst of such a tough, unforgiving life, he shared a very simple formula: "I don't know what your destiny will be, but I do know the only ones among you who will truly be happy are those who have sought and found how to serve."

If you are not drawing folks to the Lord, if you don't have others wanting to know what you have that they don't, then it might be time to look at two things. The first is your face in the mirror. Is there is a smile there? Does that image reflect happiness and joy? And second, where is your heart? Did you accept Christ as your Savior and just stop there? Maybe it is time you take a doctor's advice and get involved in serving others. Then perhaps your happiness will really show!

$\mathscr{J}$INGLE BELLS

A person's steps are made secure by the LORD when they delight in his way. —Psalm 37:23

In 1840, James S. Pierpont was asked to pen an original song for a community Thanksgiving program to be held at a church in Medford, Massachusetts. He was trying to pick out a tune on the only piano in town when he was interrupted by the happy cries of teens racing their horse-drawn sleds in the streets outside his window. Suffering from writer's block, the young man put on his coat and ducked out into the brisk November weather to observe the activities in the street. The twenty minutes he spent watching the carefree young people gave him an idea that soon became a song. Just a few weeks later, a children's choir performed Pierpont's "Jingle Bells" for the very first time. While he could sense his fun little number had made quite an impression on those lining the pews in the packed church, the amateur composer had no idea he was

about to forever alter the world's viewpoint on a much-beloved holiday.

A well-known saying goes, "You make plans, and then life gets in the way." While we might have our own ideas as to where we are going and what we want to do, we never know where God is going to take us unless we listen and follow what He tells us.

Consider Saul of Tarsus. He had a mission, and he was determined to see that mission through. Saul never could have guessed that pushing down a path to destroy all of Christianity would take him to a destination where, with a new name—Paul—he would be the guiding force behind the growth of the Christian faith. Life got in the way.

When she was in college, well-known country-music entertainer Reba McEntire had her life planned out as well. She was going to be a school teacher and hoped to coach high school basketball. Then she sang a song, and everything changed. Life got in the way.

James Pierpont wrote a song for the Thanksgiving season. That song's debut was deemed such a great success that the choir performed it again during the church's Christmas celebration. Visitors from New York and Boston, having not heard the song some weeks before, thought it had been written for Christmas, and they took it back to the cities with that in mind. Within a decade, the images Pierpont captured in his lyrics were being used on Christmas cards and holiday paintings. And snow, a one-horse open sleigh, and all the rural imagery that went with those scenes came to define Christmas all over the world.

God has a plan for your life. Are you listening for His call? Are you allowing Him to override your personal plans to open the door for something far greater? Or are you fighting Him every step of the way? Today is the time to listen to God and see if He is directing you to a place where your talents can change not just your life for the better but other lives too. No one could have predicted what would happen with Saul, Reba, or "Jingle Bells," and no one can predict where you will end up if you let God lead the way.

WHITE CHRISTMAS

Then the peace of God that exceeds all understanding will keep your hearts and minds safe in Christ Jesus. —Philippians 4:7

The dictionary defines *peace* as "a state of quiet or tranquility." In our modern world, few of us ever can get away from the noise that seemingly consumes our lives. So we have very few outwardly tranquil moments. As there are wars going on each second of every day, and battles being fought at work and home over often-trivial matters that tear at the very fabric of our hearts and minds, where can we really find peace?

In 1941, Irving Berlin penned a complete musical score for Bing Crosby's feature film *Holiday Inn*. Berlin thought most of his efforts for this project were pretty solid, but he believed his Christmas number to be weak. He brought it to Crosby with some hesitation and warned the singer the song was likely not up to the standards needed for use in the film. Bing listened to Berlin sing "White Christmas" and smiled. While the composer may have not realized it, the singer knew this number had "hit" written all over it.

A few weeks later on Christmas Eve, Crosby's mood had changed. Like millions of other unsure Americans, he was dealing with his country suddenly immersed in World War II. As peace was now nothing more than a memory, Crosby opted to debut a song embracing all the hopes and wishes for peace on his national radio show. That number would become the largest seller in recording history.

Those who first heard "White Christmas" on that radio broadcast yearned for all the things that defined Christmas, from snow to decorations to greeting cards. Yet, most of all, listeners wanted once more to experience peace on earth and good will toward men.

Irving Berlin thought he had failed when he wrote "White Christmas," but Bing Crosby's acceptance and enthusiasm for the song assured the composer he had succeeded. That success brought Berlin a sense of temporary peace, but a lasting peace can only be realized when we get past the nature of man. The peace that exceeds all understanding comes not in just accepting Christ as our Savior but in embracing the lessons He taught us in Scripture. Maybe the

best place to begin to gain this kind of trust and knowledge is in studying each of Jesus' parables. In those lessons, the master teacher shows us what is important and what is not. Knowing what makes a difference in God's world opens up a chance to find peace in our world.

In many cases, we can't experience the magic of a white Christmas without moving to a different location. It also takes moving toward God to experience real peace in life. The essence of peace is found in knowing that God is in control and trusting Him to handle the issues that are too big for us. If we can take this step, no matter the situation around us, then we will experience warmth, security, and hope beyond even our wildest dreams.

Amazing Grace

We have the same faithful spirit as what is written in scripture: I had faith, and so I spoke. We also have faith, and so we also speak. —2 Corinthians 4:13

In 1748, John Newton was one of the most unsavory characters in the world. He was a hard-drinking, often-violent sailor who served on the lowest of all vessels—a slave ship. Coming home to England from a voyage that delivered enslaved human cargo to North America, the English sailor and his shipmates found themselves at the mercy of an Atlantic hurricane. Suddenly facing what they believed was a horrible death, the ship's crew turned to Newton and begged him to pray. Remembering the example of his mother, the rough, vulgar sailor bowed his head. As the storm violently rocked the ship, Newton asked for mercy. Within moments, the tempest calmed, and the man who never had put much stock in prayer found himself with something to think about as the ship continued its journey.

Many turn to prayer only during a crisis. Communication with God, therefore, often feels strained and unnatural. Surely it was just that for John Newton more than two hundred fifty years ago as he pleaded for his life in the midst of a storm. When that calamity ended, there can be little doubt that his next prayer, one of thankfulness, came much easier. Yet, in spite of his deliverance, the coarse man did not immediately turn his life around. He continued his sinful ways for several more years before fully understanding and accepting the grace that had been shown to him during his moment of greatest tragedy.

Many of us are like John Newton on that stormy day. We acknowledge God when we are in trouble and then dismiss Him when we are sailing on calm seas. Thus our relationship with God is distant, and our full potential can never be realized.

Today we remember John Newton not for the infamous exploits of his sinful life but for his words spoken from a pulpit. More than three decades after his first prayer, Newton shared his testimony with his congregation. Those words became a hymn that likely has led to more people coming to know the Lord than any sermon ever given. When the old sailor penned "Amazing Grace," he was writing

from the heart. He knew that even the most despica-
ble life could be turned around through the miracle
of faith. After all, there was no one who had been any
worse than Newton himself.

Prayer is for more than times of great need; it is the
conduit we can and should use each day in order to
chart a course through storms and into safe waters.
As John Newton proved, there is no life that is so far
gone it can't be saved, and the testimony of even the
once-vilest sinner can be used for something incredible. In fact, it would be Newton, the former slave
trader turned Anglican pastor, who would help start
a movement that would free millions from the bonds
of slavery. John Newton knew amazing grace and
shared it. You can too. Who knows what incredible
things you can accomplish? And it all could begin
with a prayer.

I WILL ALWAYS LOVE YOU

As the Father loved me, I too have loved you. Remain in my love. —John 15:9

Over the course of the last thirty-five years, "I Will Always Love You" has become one of the most-recognized ballads in music history. Yet when Dolly Parton penned this much-beloved song, it was not intended to be a hit single. It was written as a thank you for a man who had noted her talent when no one else would even give her the time of day. The tall, thin singer from West Plains, Missouri, Porter Wagoner, gave the diminutive blonde singer from east Tennessee her first break by featuring her on his syndicated TV program, *The Porter Wagoner Show*. He then took her into the recording studio, where they teamed for several hit duets. Thanks to this exposure, Parton slowly emerged as a solo force on the country music charts. In 1974, Parton sensed it was time to move on and fly solo. Realizing that Wagoner might be hurt by her move toward independence, she penned "I Will Always Love You" as way of showing her appreciation for all her mentor had done for her. Without meaning to do so, Dolly wrote one of the most famous thank you notes in history. Not only would it top the charts for Parton but also for pop star Whitney Houston.

From the moment the nails were hammered into Christ's hands, there was no doubt that He would always love us and that His love was not limited by time or earthly bounds. That love is freely given to us when we accept Jesus as our Savior and will continue to pour into our souls long after we have left this world. In her signature song, Dolly Parton wrote about the dynamic force that is human love, but the love Christ showed when He died on the cross goes so much deeper than any of us can fathom. Even though it may not be about godly love, there is a powerful lesson in Parton's composition that Christians should embrace as they meet the challenges of everyday life.

"I Will Always Love You" was written as a musical thank you. Maybe you can't write a song or a poem, but there are probably people all around you who have provided you with guidance, inspiration, love, and assurance. They have given to you with their heart and bodies. They have sacrificed so you could achieve. They believed in your potential even as you fought with your own doubts. They deserve to know and hear your thanks.

Today is the perfect time to jot down a thank you of your own composition to someone who has been there for you. Spell out what their gifts meant to you. Tell them how your life was changed due to something they did. Prove to them that investing in you was something you noticed and appreciated.

After you mail that thank you to the person who paved the way for you to achieve spiritual or physical growth, then it is time to bow your head and acknowledge the Lord who has vowed to always love you. Through your words and your actions, you can show that you not only accept His gift of love but also share it with all those you meet.

YOU ARE
MY SUNSHINE

*God said, "Let there be light." And so light appeared. God saw
how good the light was. God separated the light from the darkness. God named the light Day and the darkness Night.*
—Genesis 1:3-5

"You Are My Sunshine" possesses a near-perfect
combination of an infectious melody coupled with
simple lyrics; therefore, it is almost impossible to forget. In the more than seven decades since it was
penned by Paul Rice, it has become an American
musical standard, and it has been recorded hundreds
of times and tallied millions of dollars in royalties. It
was Louisianan Jimmy Davis who first made "Sunshine" a huge hit, and since 1940, a long list of other
artists has also recorded this country classic. Yet
when he died, the song's composer had little to show
for his greatest work. Just before Davis recorded it,
Rice sold all rights to "Sunshine" for $17.50.

Humans often are shortsighted when it comes to

their choices in life. We often sacrifice the future in return for the immediate rewards in the present. In Paul Rice's case, he sold all his rights to "You Are My Sunshine" for literally "a song" in order to fuel his addiction to alcohol. Countless others have done the same thing. We are a people who desire to experience the moment rather than plan for a lifetime. The Bible is filled with such folks.

There is light in this world so that we can make the best decisions. Light allows us to clearly see the solid ground, the best pathway, and right from wrong, and our choices in those areas define us. God didn't create the light just for the world; He created light for our souls as well. And when there is light in your life, you not only make the wiser decisions but also become a beacon for others who are struggling like Paul Rice.

When we allow the light of the Lord to shine in our world, it allows us to see the blessings around us as well as illuminate the very things that are holding us back from having that happiness each moment of each day. As you sing "You Are My Sunshine," as those easy-to-recall lyrics run through your mind, take stock of your life. What is holding you back? Do you have an addiction that is causing you to be shortsighted? Are you selling the promise of bright tomorrows for the immediate pleasures of today? Are you investing everything you have in the moment or in the future? As you look at your answers, you might come to realize what is taking your sunshine away.

$\mathcal{J}$ESUS LOVES ME

But this is precisely what is written: God has prepared things for those who love him that no eye has seen, or ear has heard, or that haven't crossed the mind of any human being. —1 Corinthians 2:9

In 1860, Anna Warner, using the pseudonym Amy Lothrop, penned a best-selling novel entitled *Say and Seal*. Today that book has slipped so far from the public consciousness that few have ever heard of, much less read, what was the top seller of its time. Yet thanks to a single deeply emotional moment covering less than a page, *Say and Seal* has cemented itself into basic Christian history like no other passage from any other American book ever penned. How is this possible?

In an attempt to comfort the dying child she inserted into her story, Anna Warner had the lead character, Mr. Linden, recite a poem. The poem she wrote for that occasion so moved songwriter William Bradbury that he added music and published it as "Jesus Loves Me." This elementary children's hymn was the most popular new song introduced during the Civil War. Yet that was just the beginning. In the past one hundred and seventy years, "Jesus Loves Me" has become the best-known, most-translated piece of Christian music in the world.

The story of how this song has become such an important part of history is one of the most profound lessons ever presented. One small passage in a book meant only to set the tone for a single scene became greater than any other act in Anna Warner's life. She had no way of knowing what her poem would come to mean to hundreds of millions. She never intended for it to strike such a chord. She simply wrote it only as a plot device.

That is the way life is. The things we often think are important fade as quickly as we do them. It is the little things that tend to make the greatest impact. Few of those around Jesus would have guessed that today we would be talking about and learning from Christ's visit with the woman at the well or His call to Zacchaeus to come down from the tree. At the time Jesus did these simple acts of kindness I am sure they must have seemed like "throwaway" moments to the disciples. But what an impact they had!

As you sing through "Jesus Loves Me," as you consider its simple message, think about the most

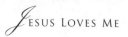

important lessons you have been taught in life. Frame them in the context of how they happened. Did those who touched you at those times realize they were making a lasting impact? Now is the moment to realize that you can make this same kind of impact in the little things you do each day. No act of kindness is too small, no word is without meaning, and no display of love is futile when it reaches the heart of at least one person.

DEEP AND WIDE

You must follow the LORD your God alone! Revere him! Follow his commandments! Obey his voice! Worship him! Cling to him—no other! —Deuteronomy 13:4

We when go against our nation's laws, there are almost always consequences. We face judgment and often must pay penalties. In many cases, the rulings laid down for walking on the wrong side of justice are stiff and unforgiving. Even though those who aren't caught pay a high price as they spend the rest of their lives looking over their shoulder, dreading the day their crimes are brought to light.

In the world of faith, there are also laws that have been laid down by God. And just like in the real world, there are many Christians who have great difficulty walking the walk of faith. Though they know the right road is straight and narrow, many give in to the temptations and veer off course. By the time they look up, they are miles from where they are supposed to be traveling. The most common term for this is backsliding, and it is hardly a new phenomenon.

Adam and Eve were backsliders veering from the road simply by disobeying one elementary rule God had given them. David, Samson, and a host of others strayed from the path as well. Most of them stepped into the world of darkness by putting themselves and their needs first. As we read the stories of the lives of those who became our biblical heroes, we find that each of them paid dearly for straying from what he or she knew was the charted course.

If in civil or criminal matters you draw the wrong judge, then you will find little forgiveness or understanding. We are therefore fortunate that our God is a forgiving and loving God. Rather than condemn us for our weaknesses, He recognizes them. Rather than doom us for being imperfect, He offers us compassion and the promise of an eternal life. So while the way of righteousness might be narrow, God's love and forgiveness knows no bounds.

Children learn about the enormity of God's love early on when they sing the old vacation Bible school standard "Deep and Wide." We don't know who wrote the music or the lyrics, but the message found in "Deep and Wide" is what sets Christianity apart: the love that flows from God's fountain never stops.

Thus, He is always ready to welcome the straying soul back to His flock.

While we tend to forgive our biblical heroes for their weaknesses, we often can't seem to offer that same forgiveness to our family, our friends, our business associates, or even our country's leaders. If we truly believe that God's love is deep and wide, then ours must be as well. We, therefore, must stop judging and start loving.

Today is a day to forgive and to welcome back into our lives someone who has strayed. We need to offer them the same kind of acceptance and compassion God has offered to us when we have messed up. When we forgive and love someone who has hurt us, we become more like Jesus. And isn't that a goal we all want to claim?

$\mathcal{Y}$ou Raise Me Up

Let's also think about how to motivate each other to show love and to do good works. Don't stop meeting together with other believers, which some people have gotten into the habit of doing. Instead, encourage each other, especially as you see the day drawing near. —Hebrews 10:24-25

Salvation is a personal experience. It happens when God enters the heart of a single individual. But living a Christian life should not be a solitary adventure. It should be shared! Those who worship Christ are, therefore, meant to come together to sing, pray, and lift each other up.

In 2002, Norwegian composer Rolf Lovland created a melody inspired by the ancient Irish folk standard "Danny Boy." As his tune had its roots in a musical number born in the Emerald Isle, it seemed only natural that Rolf would turn to an Irish woman for the lyrics. Brenda Graham took Lovland's touching and uplifting melody and married it to words that resolutely declare that we never do anything alone. This song, as much as any recent composition, defines the importance of compassion and inspiration when achieving anything worthwhile.

"You Raise Me Up" has never topped the rock charts, though it did hit #1 on Adult Contemporary playlists, nor been adopted as the signature song of any popular musical artist, and yet it has defied the odds by becoming one of this century's best-known and most-loved songs. How has it accomplished this seemingly impossible feat? Perhaps because everyone has someone who was there for him or her in the defining moments of life. The song's deeply personal point of view is likely the reason that in just a decade, "You Raise Me Up" has become a staple on television talent programs and has been performed on stages, in churches, and in schools all around the globe.

In the Bible's first verses, we read that God saw it was not good for Adam to be alone. It is also not good for us to be alone. We need the support of others, and we should seek out a place of worship where we feel as if we are a part of the family of God. And we must find those who are not a part of the body, who are alone, perhaps sick or scared, the forgotten, the lost, the hurting, and the shut-in, and bring them into our family.

In Paul's letters to the early Christian churches, he writes of his own "raise me up" experiences. In fact, he specifically thanks church members for being there for him in times of great need. His words continually reinforce that, while coming to the Lord is a personal experience, doing God's work is a group activity.

Each one of us needs to meet regularly with other Christians. We need to share our joys and our fears. Through participating in churches, Bible study groups, missions, and outreach programs, we realize the joy of meeting others' needs. The simple truth is that being with others allows us to raise up the least of these when they need it the most.

$\mathscr{I}$F I CAN DREAM

May the God of endurance and encouragement give you the same attitude toward each other, similar to Christ Jesus' attitude. That way you can glorify the God and Father of our Lord Jesus Christ together with one voice. So welcome each other, in the same way that Christ also welcomed you, for God's glory.
—Romans 15:5-7

In 1968, Elvis Presley returned to live performance for the first time in seven years. His network television special would include songs from his career as well as spotlight Presley in a gospel music set. But as he rehearsed with his band, the King of Rock and Roll seemed more troubled than excited. During a break, the topic of his concern stunned songwriter Walter Earl Brown. In the wake of the assassinations of Martin Luther King and Bobby Kennedy, Presley was worried about what was happening to America. Elvis was haunted by the fact the doors to hope and compassion were closing rather than opening, and the country he loved was becoming darker rather than brighter. Inspired by the singer's concerns, Brown went back and reread Martin Luther King's famous "I Have a Dream" speech. Using that speech as his inspiration, the songwriter created the social ballad "If I Can Dream." Over the objections of his manager and the network, Elvis chose the number to conclude his NBC comeback special. Presley's performance of the song was so powerful that it left even the entertainer's band and backup singers in tears. It also set millions to asking, "Why can't that dream come true?"

When confronted by racial intolerance, poverty, or other social issues, most people just shrug and use the excuse that it has always been that way and always will be. They offer no hope at all. Time and time again, Christ pointed out that we are all God's children. Our backgrounds or race should never come into play in how we perceive others. And yet we live in a world where dreams are crushed and potential is lost because we find ways to separate people into groups rather than bring them together.

Christ was the great equalizer. He spelled out the brotherhood of man in ways that had never been considered before His teachings. Jesus knew no prejudice. When He looked at the young or the old, what He saw was potential, and what He exuded was compassion. His teaching was so radical that He turned the world upside down and kick-started the dreamers who believed this could be a better place for all people.

A key line in the song "If I Can Dream" begins, "There must be lights burning brighter somewhere." The light that is missing in so many parts of the world is not fueled by electricity but by faith, understanding, hope, and the desire to remake the world into a better place. You can make an impact by believing; as Christ taught time and time again, you are a conduit for His love. Become more like Jesus and you will be colorblind and naturally embrace everyone as your brother and sister. Becoming the light that is burning brighter is the perfect way to share your faith as you light the way for dreams to come true.

$\mathcal{S}$HE LOVES YOU

God is love, and those who remain in love remain in God and God remains in them. —1 John 4:16

After years of struggling to find an audience, the Beatles were just beginning to take off in Europe when Paul McCartney heard an American teen idol's latest hit single. Bobby Rydell's "Forget Him" struck McCartney as being very unusual in that its lyrics, written in the third person, urged a brokenhearted man to forget the girl who had just dumped him. McCartney seized on that theme and turned it around. Rather than giving advice to move on, Paul wrote a song that begged the brokenhearted man to continue to push forward in his attempts to win his girlfriend's heart. "She Loves You" was an original idea voicing a universal message that would become one of the Beatles' first worldwide hits.

Because he was English, McCartney likely was not aware of the term "cheerleader." If he had been born and raised in the United States, then he would have realized that the third-person voice in the Beatles' hit single was filling that role. The message found in the song was to have faith, don't give up; even if she doesn't realize it yet, she does love you. And that is the message most brokenhearted lovers want to hear.

The old gospel music standard "Farther Along" embraces a similar theme, but in this case, the hurting soul is not voicing concern about a love bound by the rules of earth but of the love of God for His children. Job likely would have identified with "Farther Along" as he looked toward heaven and wondered why he was being so mistreated. If you glance around today, then you will find scores of people who are also asking that same question. If God loves us and we are following His ways, then why do these bad things happen to us? When those questions are asked, when those doubts are voiced, and when times get the toughest is when a cheerleader is needed to step forward and assure those hurting that God hurts with them.

Probably few people had as much pain and suffering fall into their lives as did Paul. His letters to the various Christian churches of his day reveal the extent of his trials. Yet while his words often show him in prison or in poor health, they also reveal something else of great importance. Time and time again, Paul declared he made it through the darkest days in his life because a friend loved him enough to be there for him.

Many people have a fear of reaching out to those in pain. The most common excuse is, "I wouldn't know what to say." If you truly believe God is alive and living in your heart, then you must also believe that the words will be given to you when you need them. And maybe your words aren't needed at all; maybe all that is needed is your presence. By being there, you assure those in pain that God does care and that He still loves them. If a great man of faith like Paul benefited and was inspired by the presence of a Christian friend, then surely your compassion and touch also will show those suffering in your life that "the Lord still loves them too."

MOON RIVER

I came so that they could have life—indeed, so that they could live life to the fullest. —John 10:10

In 1960, famed songsmiths Johnny Mercer and Henry Mancini were assigned to write music for the Hollywood film *Breakfast at Tiffany's*. Their job proved to be a great challenge, as one of the songs was to be sung by Audrey Hepburn. Hepburn's range was so severely limited that it was painfully obvious she was never cut out to be a musical performer. Therefore the song had to be simple, easy to sing, and undemanding, but it also still had to move the film's plot forward. With that framework in mind, Mercer and Mancini created a number about a holly plant that the studio quickly rejected. The discouraged duo went back to the drawing boards and reworked their song into an ode about a river. Hepburn's performance of "Moon River" was adequate, but that didn't keep one Paramount Pictures executive from noting that the performance ruined the

movie's pace and demanding it be deleted from the film. If director Blake Edwards hadn't insisted it be retained, then "Moon River" would never have been heard, much less nominated for an Oscar.

First impressions might be lasting, but they are often, as in the case of "Moon River," woefully inaccurate. When he first tried out for his high-school basketball team, Michael Jordan was cut. Elvis Presley failed so miserably when he made his debut at the Grand Ole Opry that he was told he'd have a brighter future driving a truck. Harry S. Truman might be revered as one of America's great presidents, but as a businessman, he went bankrupt. It took the pioneer missionary William Carey more than five years of work to lead one person to the Lord in India. And imagine for a moment how everyone must have viewed the potential of the child named Helen Keller.

People should not be judged on first impressions or one experience. Just as Christ never gives up on anyone, we must not either. God has given us many chances. He saw our potential even when we did not see it ourselves. He probably even sent someone to encourage us when we needed it most. Now is the time to do the same for others. Those we view as "the least of these" might well turn out to be the next great entertainer, scientist, writer, or leader. We also might just be the person who brings light to someone like Saul. Imagine, God has placed within us that kind of power. But having it and not being an encouraging force who sees potential where others see failure means we are not living life to the fullest.

Consider the first impressions of Jesus. Simply put, Christ didn't live up to expectations. Those looking for a messiah wanted a warrior to overthrow the government of Rome, but what they got was a teacher who preached the brotherhood of all men. He didn't offer to overturn governments; instead, He tossed out ancient rules and preached about love. He challenged those in authority not with a sword but with parables. The establishment of that day viewed Jesus as a pretender and an abject failure, but, my, how those viewpoints have changed. Aren't you glad that first impressions are not the final impression God has of us?

$\mathcal{B}$LUE MOON

So, faith comes from listening, but it's listening by means of Christ's message. —Romans 10:17

"Blue Moon" stands apart as the only song written by famed Broadway tunesmiths Richard Rodgers and Lorenz Hart that was not intended for one of their musicals. Yet in their stellar careers, perhaps none of their vast legions of hits has been sung by more people in more varied styles than this lonesome ballad. Remarkably, the song almost never made it into a recording session.

It began life as a number entitled "Make Me a Star" and was intended for a 1933 Jean Harlow film. When it was dropped in favor of another composer's offering, Rodgers and Hart retuned to the studio and reworked the lyrics. For the next two years, the duo kept playing with the song's words and pitched the number for use in a wide variety of films, only to be rejected time and time again. Finally, in 1935, with new words centering on a lonely blue moon, it became a number-one hit for the Casa Loma Orchestra. From that humble beginning, "Blue Moon" has sold tens of millions of records and landed scores of times on pop, blues, country, rock, and easy listening charts.

Rodgers and Hart were sure they had a winner when they created the original melody. They had confidence that it was a tune the world would love. The problem they had centered on the way the song was delivered. It took the team several years and scores of rewrites to come up with a musical vehicle that was accepted.

Over the course of a decade, I tried to interest publishers in a book called *The Stories Behind the Best-Loved Songs of Christmas*. Though I constantly reworked the idea and the proposal, the book was rejected twenty-seven times. Yet, I continued to believe in that idea so much I kept pitching. I finally found an editor who would listen. I convinced her of the strength of my concept, and she went to bat for me. The book that resulted became a bestseller and spawned a dozen sequels. The key to success was not giving up.

The thing that keeps most Christians from sharing the good news is rejection. They believe in the message but are not confident in their ability to share it.

Many who find the courage to talk about their faith to a friend or family member and have that testimony rejected often clam up and never make a second attempt.

If you truly believe Christ is your Savior and that His message is something that not only would save the souls of others but also enhance the joy in their earthly lives, then you must share that news. Keeping it to yourself would be not only selfish but also contrary to everything Christ taught. Your timing will not always be perfect, and you will no doubt experience rejection, but like Rodgers and Hart, you can't let that stop you. If you strongly believe in the message, then you just need to keep working until you find an approach for successfully sharing it. Don't forget, most initially rejected Jesus, but look how many have come to accept Him now.

$\mathscr{S}$TARDUST

Fetch the fattened calf and slaughter it. We must celebrate with feasting because this son of mine was dead and has come back to life! He was lost and is found!' And they began to celebrate.
—Luke 15:23-24

Few composers penned as many timeless classics as Hoagy Carmichael. The Indiana-born songwriter's brilliant mind gave the world such unforgettable songs as "Georgia on My Mind," "Up the Lazy River," "Heart and Soul," and "The Nearness of You." But it would be one of the lawyer-turned-tunesmith's first published works that would come to be regarded as his greatest. Carmichael was playing around on a piano at the Keuka Hotel on Finger Lake in western New York, when he created a magical tune he called "Stardust." Throughout the 1920s and early 1930s, the song would be cut a dozen times, and that was just the beginning. Though it has been recorded by legends including Bing Crosby, Frank Sinatra, Nat King Cole, Billie Holiday, and

Doris Day, no singer has ever created the definitive version of this song—but that isn't keeping people from continuing to try. Thus, "Stardust" remains one of a handful of almost ninety-year-old American tunes that is still consistently recorded and performed.

Timeless classics are few and far between. In the world of music, today's hits often are dismissed and forgotten in less than a decade. Therefore it takes something incredibly special to stand the test of time. While "Stardust" has earned that status for more than eight decades of popularity, that pales when compared to the timeless value found in parables of Christ.

When Jesus shared the story of the prodigal son, it was aimed at an audience that recognized the time-honored code of Jewish inheritance law. Those who listened to Christ knew that the firstborn was given two-thirds of the estate and the next son was to be given one-third. They fully understood the disrespect the younger son showed when demanding the father give him his part of the estate before the older man had died. And if the story had ended with the father handing the younger son his due, perhaps the parable would have been forgotten in time. But Christ was not talking to just the small audience that had gathered around Him that day, He was speaking to all of humanity. This story lives on because the son came home in disgrace and was welcomed by his father. Therefore the moral was not as much about squandering an inheritance as it was about the timeless values of forgiveness, acceptance, and redemption.

Jesus' words are as powerful and meaningful today as when He first said them. The lessons He taught defy time itself. More than two thousand years of history have not weakened their message. And no preacher, teacher, or missionary has ever been able to put his or her exclusive stamp on what Jesus shared. These parables are for each one of us to claim as our own, to use as inspiration, and they are a vehicle to take us closer to an understanding of God and His will for our lives.

$\mathcal{Y}$ESTERDAY

Jesus Christ is the same yesterday, today, and forever!
—*Hebrews 13:8*

Jesus was someone who turned the world upside down. He asked folks to give up thousands of years of time-honored traditions and home in on things that sounded completely foreign. He asked people to share what they had with the poor, to quit judging and start accepting, to realize that God was the God for all people, and then He had the gall to suggest that forgiveness was far more important than judgment. To the establishment of that day, this kind of radical talk was deeply disturbing. How could they forget the ancient rules and still hope to walk with God?

Two thousand years later, men and women are still frightened by change. At times, people become so overwhelmed by the demands of change that they grow depressed and look back at a time when life seemed so much simpler and better. In fact, that kind of thinking inspired one of the greatest and most thoughtful ballads of the 1960s.

After years of working just outside the spotlight, in 1964, the Beatles were the hottest entertainers on the planet. Though they had dreamed of fame for years, little did they realize the price they would have to pay when it came to them. Their fast-paced schedule, the screaming and demanding fans, the grueling travel, and the newfound wealth took a toll on the boys from Liverpool. No longer could they just hang out with friends or walk the streets. Even eating in a restaurant proved a challenge.

Paul McCartney was in the midst of living this demanding new life when he got up from his sleep and dashed out the notes to a melody that became a haunting ballad he initially called "Scrambled Eggs." It was sometime later, during a trip to Portugal, when he finally created the lyrics and changed the song's name to "Yesterday." Ironically, except for McCartney, the other Beatles weren't impressed by the music or the song's theme. They argued "Yester-day" represented too great a change from what had made them famous. McCartney stuck to his guns, and the song that looked back to when "troubles seemed so far away" became a hit.

Just as George, Ringo, and John may have feared

changing music styles might hurt their careers, many of us are overwhelmed by all kinds of change. We fear expanding technology, a career shift, a loss in the family, or even the outcome of a political race, and thus, we long for the way things used to be.

Two thousand years ago, the guiding force in new Christians' lives was Jesus. His words directed the way they responded to everything. And through all of the incredible changes that have taken place since then, Jesus, the man who brought great change during His days on earth, has been that one unchanging constant. His parables, His simple rules, and His directive to love one another still hold true. And if we remember that biblical fact, then we have no reason to fear today or long for yesterday.

WRITE THE SONGS

Shout triumphantly to the LORD, all the earth! —Psalm 100:1

In 1975, Barry Manilow was a pop music sensation. In the age of heavy rock bands, he was a throwback: a crooner who played the piano. He also was recognized as one of the best new composers in pop music. Late in that year, Manilow hesitantly cut a song that had been penned by a popular musician from a group known as America's band.

Bruce Johnston helped define the surf sound when he and the Beach Boys cut a long series of hits throughout the 1960s. Though overshadowed by the writing and arranging of Brian Wilson, Johnston also had a hand in developing the legendary group's unique sounds. In the early seventies, Johnston wrote "I Write the Songs." The Beach Boys passed on Johnston's composition, but later, Clive Davis at Arista Records discovered the unappreciated ballad and insisted Manilow cut it. Davis's instincts were spot-on, as "I Write the Songs" would become a number one hit in January 1976, and it was chosen as the Grammy winner for Song of the Year in 1977.

Manilow was initially uncomfortable with "I Write the Songs" because he felt listeners might somehow see it as his claiming to be the world's greatest composer. Johnston urged Manilow to take a closer look at the lyrics. The Beach Boy was not writing about a songwriter but about God. In other words, the lyrics were crafted as if the Lord were singing them.

Over the years, the uplifting strains combined with its joyous lyrics have made "I Write the Songs" an important part of the fabric of American music. Yet, just as Manilow initially missed its subtle salute to God, most who listen to the hit song have not caught the message that was so wonderfully crafted into its words. That is hardly surprising as most people also fail to note the work of the Lord in the world and in their lives.

God's incredible musical productions are all around us and are begging us to join them in song. When you see the myriad colors of autumn or the flowers of spring, they are a part of the melody that the Lord composed for us—as is the cry of a newborn child or the smile of grandparent. So too is every good deed and act of love.

As we go through our lives, what is the melody

that comes out of our mouths? Does it reflect the joy of being a part of God's creation or does it lack His inspiring touch? If we know the Lord, then we should have His Spirit of love in our songs of life, and we should mirror Him in our words and actions. As Jesus said, we must become like Him. When we do, then others will want to know what we have that they don't. What is it that makes us so different, so joyful, so filled with hope? When asked, we can explain that we know the one who wrote the songs that have been making the world sing since the beginning of time.

$\mathcal{T}$HE ROSE

The grass dries up; the flower withers, but our God's word will exist forever. —Isaiah 40:8

Perhaps no flower has been as immortalized in literature as has the rose. It is so much a symbol of devotion that it has come to represent love on the most romantic of all days—Valentine's Day. Though it doesn't expressly say so in the Bible, Jesus is often referred to as "the Rose of Sharon" (see Song of Solomon 2:1). It was said that Sharon was the most beautiful and peaceful place on earth, and Christ, as the rose, therefore stood for God's most glorious and loving creation.

Roses, by nature, are delicate. They grace us with their blooms for just a short while and then, before we have time to fully appreciate them, they wilt and disappear. In a very real sense, that is the way of each of our lives. We race through time thinking our days on earth stretch out forever and yet, in the blink of an eye, the carefree spring of our youth has given way to the cold winter winds of old age. On earth, nothing, not even man, stays beautiful and blooms forever.

Isaiah speaks of God's word being eternal. But what does that mean? Are we to think of ink on pages or a speech once spoken and now just a memory? Hardly! It means that God is the one thing that will never die.

For the Christian, the promise of a life without ending was proven with Christ's resurrection. Thus the Rose of Sharon did not fade but rather remains as beautiful, fragrant, and strong today as it was yesterday. A million years from now it will be blooming as well. But what does that mean to us?

One of the most hauntingly beautiful songs released in the 1970s was "The Rose." Written by Amanda McBroom, "The Rose" is an attempt to explain love from a number of different points of view. The ballad came to be known and much beloved when Bette Midler sang it in the movie that shared its name. In McBroom's composition, there is one line that jumps out to all who have sung or heard "The Rose." The line speaks of man's greatest fear: "And the soul afraid of dyin' that never learns to live."

I once watched in amazement as a friend lived

with terminal cancer. In spite of an illness that was taking her life when she was barely thirty, she seemed in full bloom—like a perfect red rose. The secret to her happiness was that she realized each earthly moment was a gift God intended her to embrace and enjoy. Yet because she also knew that Jesus had died for her, she didn't have to worry about death.

Once we get over the fear of death, once we can embrace the promise that the word is eternal and God intends us to be with Him forever, then life on earth becomes so much better because we know that even in our worst times the rose will return to grace and inspire us with its fragile beauty.

$\mathcal{H}$ALLELUJAH CHORUS

We know that God works all things together for good for the ones who love God, for those who are called according to his purpose. —Romans 8:28

Imagine having lost fame. It happens all the time. Each year, actors, singers, athletes, and even business people who once were on top of the world slip into obscurity. After years of having everyone knowing their names and treating them as if they were royalty, they find themselves having very little value. In our modern world, there is a term for this. It is called "when your fifteen minutes of fame are up." But the phenomenon of the one-hit wonder didn't begin in the information age. Fame and fortune have always been fleeting.

German-born George Handel worked his way up from obscurity to being the toast of London. The talented composer specialized in oratorios. These dramatic musical presentations of biblical stories became the most popular music of the early 1700s, with

royalty and commoners alike waiting breathlessly to hear each one Handel produced. But musical tastes change, and songwriters who don't change with them usually are dismissed as quickly as they were discovered. Less than a decade after having been on the Buckingham Palace guest list, Handel was a debt-ridden pauper living alone and afraid in a tiny shack on the wrong side of town. He prayed nightly his creditors would not find him and toss him in debtors' prison.

In August 1742, a letter arrived written by a man many deemed crazy. Yet as Charles Jennens was one of the few friends Handel had left in the world, he carefully opened the envelope and read Jennens's suggestion for a new oratorio. Over the course of the next three weeks, the composer wrote a musical that he was sure would never find an audience. He'd just finished it when another friend asked Handel to help with a charity concert raising money for a hospital serving the poorest of the poor. Handel took his new music with him and presented it at that concert for the very first time. Handel's *Messiah* initially raised a huge sum of money for the charity and then revived the popularity of the oratorio style of music and the composer who wrote them better than anyone. Handel was once again on top of the world.

There is a great lesson in the story behind this incredible piece of music. That lesson goes beyond the fragility of worldly fame. It involves God using people whom others have written off as having no value. Handel was one of these. Supposedly his day was past. Then there was Charles Jennens, a man everyone thought was, at the least, eccentric and, at the most, insane. God was able to use Jennens to rescue Handel. And then Handel was able to employ the idea Jennens gave him to create a musical piece that generated gifts for a charity that served people just like him. Since that time, *Messiah* has raised more money for "the least of these" than any other music ever written.

No person is so insignificant that he or she can't be used by God. No person is too old, sick, or frail to make an impact. And just as the Lord remembered Handel, He will remember you in your greatest time of need. Don't give up on the people the world dismisses, and don't give up on the Lord.

ℬLUE SKIES

In the same way, let your light shine before people, so they can see the good things you do and praise your Father who is in heaven. —Matthew 5:16

For as long as man has been looking toward the heavens, clear skies have always seemed to brighten moods. In 1926, Broadway's greatest songwriting team, Rodgers and Hart, added a newly composed Irving Berlin song based on the theme of clear skies to their musical production *Betsy*. The show lasted barely a month and has been long forgotten, but the song "Blue Skies" made such a powerful impression that it became a number-one hit on the popular music charts, was featured in the first talking motion picture, *The Jazz Singer*, and would become the basis for a 1946 Bing Crosby and Fred Astaire film. By the 1970s, "Blue Skies" had been recorded hundreds of times and Willie Nelson even rode the old number to the top of the charts again. So while Rodgers and Hart's *Betsy* was quickly forgotten, the song the composers added to their show at the last minute, Irving Berlin's "Blue Skies," continues to make millions smile each day.

One of the song's most beloved lines goes, "Bluebirds singing a song—Nothing but bluebirds all day long." The bluebird was the symbol of happiness to many Native American tribes. Just seeing a bluebird was a sign your troubles would soon be over. It represented hope, joy, and the promise of blessings.

Consider this for a moment. Who are the happiest people you know? Who are the folks whose smiles and twinkling eyes light up your life? And what do they have in common? In most cases, they likely feel blessed. They have God in their heart and are following Jesus' teachings. Their eyes are focused on finding ways to reach those who are going through really tough times. They also have their priorities in the proper place. Most are likely not caught up in what they have but in what they can give to others. Thus they may not have the largest bank accounts, but they do have the biggest hearts. With almost everything they do and say, they reveal the joy found in walking in Jesus' footsteps. They do what they can do and let God handle the rest. Simply put, they don't worry about things they can't fix. And when you live that way, there are a lot of blue skies to enjoy.

Bluebirds and blue skies have no magical power, but there is a mood changer available to all of us at no cost. God has blessed you. At the very least, His son is a bridge to eternal life. That alone is something to smile about and celebrate. But that is just the beginning. If you pull out a piece of paper and begin to jot down your blessings, that list likely will be a long one, and each one of those is also a reason to smile.

Do you want to adopt "Blue Skies" as your theme song? Then emulate those who smile their way through lives. Today is the day to begin to give to God all the things you can't handle. With those concerns out of your life, you will find it much easier to smile at others and shine for the Lord.

Over the Rainbow

God said, "This is the symbol of the covenant that I am drawing up between me and you and every living thing with you, on behalf of every future generation. I have placed my bow in the clouds; it will be the symbol of the covenant between me and the earth." —Genesis 9:12-13

In 1939, MGM was putting the final touches on a movie based on a children's literary classic. *The Wizard of Oz* had been in the works for a long time, but production had been delayed due to story and casting problems. The studio executives initially felt they had no one in their stable of stars who could play the lead, thus they tried to work out a deal to obtain Shirley Temple from Fox Studios in a one-picture deal. As Fox also wanted MGM's top star, Jean Harlow, for one of their films, the deal was almost worked out. But when Harlow tragically died in 1937, so did MGM's chance to get the talented Temple. That led to MGM head Louis B. Mayer looking inside his own studio and taking a chance on a

teenager whose name had recently been changed from Frances Gumm to Judy Garland.

When completed, *The Wizard of Oz* was screened in a theater in San Luis Obispo, California. Audiences seemed to enjoy it, but Mayer and producer Mervyn LeRoy thought one element of the film slowed the plot down. Thus they ordered that the song "Over the Rainbow" be cut from the final print. If not for the insistence of associate producer Arthur Freed, the classic song likely never would have been heard again.

Many view church attendance in the same way as Mayer and LeRoy viewed "Over the Rainbow"—an unnecessary part of life's plot. On the surface, this belief seems understandable. People are incredibly busy. They live in a world that is whirling by at breakneck speed. Sunday morning is the one time when many have an opportunity to really rest. Yet just like *The Wizard of Oz* wouldn't be complete without Judy Garland singing "Over the Rainbow," we need a time to slow down, pray, hear God's word, and fellowship with other Christians to have a complete week. This change of pace in life's script allows us a few moments to put the other elements of our hurried life into perspective.

The Wizard of Oz became one of the most beloved

films of all time. Judy Garland's "Over the Rainbow" has come to be recognized as one of America's greatest anthems of hope and faith. In many ways, it reflects the meaning of the rainbow found in the Bible's first book. God gave us the symbol to assure us of continuing love. But to fully grasp and use that love in our lives, it helps to have a church family to celebrate our joys and provide support when things go wrong. Millions have been found comfort in the song "Over the Rainbow" and can't imagine *The Wizard of Oz* without it. Hundreds of millions have been blessed and their lives enriched by spending an hour each week with fellow Christians. The treasure promised at the end of the rainbow is most likely to be found when sitting in a pew or doing God's work.

$\mathcal{G}$OD BLESS AMERICA

Jesus answered, "I assure you, unless someone is born anew, it's not possible to see God's kingdom." Nicodemus asked, "How is it possible for an adult to be born? It's impossible to enter the mother's womb for a second time and be born, isn't it?" Jesus answered, "I assure you, unless someone is born of water and the Spirit, it's not possible to enter God's kingdom."
—John 3:3-5

In 1917, the United States entered a worldwide war with a sense of excitement and enthusiasm. Many thought the trip to Europe would be a grand adventure and a chance for young men to emerge as heroes to their country and their families. Then the effects of mustard gas, modern weapons, and hand-to-hand combat painted war as the nightmare it really was.

Knowing the risks, composer Irving Berlin joined the service to fight for his adopted homeland. But Uncle Sam opted to employ Berlin's skill as a song-writer rather than allow the talented man to take on the Germans in combat. Using only military personnel, the tunesmith created a Broadway show called *Yip Yip Yaphank* to raise money for the widows and orphans the war had created. During final rehearsals, Berlin decided one of his songs was simply too syrupy to make the grade, and he cut it. The songwriter would not even think about the number until twenty years later when Kate Smith was looking for a new patriotic song to sing to her radio audience on Armistice Day. Berlin had his secretary dig out his old tune and give it to the popular singer. Smith's arranger changed the song from a march to a ballad and in 1938 "God Bless America" finally made its debut. It was an immediate hit!

Like that song that was initially dismissed by its creator, critics and producers had also scorned Kate Smith. Smith was a large woman with a plain face. On stage, the only roles she could get were those of the fat woman comics made fun of. She was about to give up and go into nursing when radio offered her a second chance. Her robust voice and upbeat personality were perfect for the newly launched medium, and the fact she was large and plain didn't matter to those listening in their homes, offices, and cars.

Without second chances, one of America's favorite

patriotic hymns along with one of entertainment's most endearing legends would have been forever lost. Both were reborn at the right time to make dramatic imprints on the world.

Unlike the world, Jesus didn't give up on anyone based on first, second, or even third impressions. No matter our past, no matter how we had been judged by our harshest critics, no matter our size, race, or social standing, God offered and still offers a second chance at life. And the new life God has given is filled with endless potential.

It took a once rejected woman to bring "God Bless America" to life and cement it into the fabric of history. In our own lives, it took a man the world rejected to give us a second chance at living a life filled with purpose on earth and living eternally in heaven.

In the Mood

If any of you are suffering, they should pray. If any of you are happy, they should sing. —James 5:13

Countless folks put off doing things they either need or want to do because they feel it just isn't time yet. How many people do you know who have a fine set of china or silver they are keeping in their cabinets until someone special comes to visit? Do you know people who buy fancy clothes but never wear them because they are waiting for a really big event? Or how about folks who are going to get a health issue checked out just as soon as they have a break in their schedule?

There are hosts of people who put God off in the same way. They promise that they will go to church, study the Bible, or get involved in Christian outreach when the mood strikes. "I just don't feel like it right now" is the excuse pastors hear all the time.

It is easy to get in the mood to do something we really want to do. If there is a party we want to go to,

a movie we want to see, or a friend we want to hang out with, we find a way to make it happen. But try to find a moment to write a thank you note or do a favor for a neighbor and it seems almost impossible.

One of the most popular big band tunes of all times has an obscure background. No one really knows where the swinging number "In the Mood" originated. Long before it ended up in Glenn Miller's hands, it had been played by a number of Harlem bands and been recorded under a couple of different titles. Miller actually first heard the song in 1938, just when his Big Band sound was taking off, but didn't do anything with it for more than a year. The reason? Neither he nor the members of his orchestra could find the time to come up with a suitable arrangement. What finally prompted them into action was a deadline. Miller needed a new song for his August 1, 1939, recording session.

The Glenn Miller Orchestra had a long string of hits, but no one record defined their incredible sound like "In the Mood." The song is one of the few from that era that is still being recorded today. In fact, it might be as well known now as it was in when it first hit the charts seven decades ago, so it is ironic that Miller almost failed to get into the mood to arrange the number.

What are you saving for a special occasion? What are you missing by not getting in the mood? What does God have in store for you that you are simply ignoring? Is God calling you to work in your church, get involved in volunteering in the community? Is there a child who needs a mentor or an old person who needs a friend? Don't wait to get in the mood to serve the Lord. Instead, start serving God now, and you will find your mood will take you to places you never dreamed you'd go and experience happiness and satisfaction you didn't know you could have. And that is a mood you will want to sing about and share!

My BLUE HEAVEN

If God is for us, who is against us? —Romans 8:31

In the 1920s, Walter Donaldson wrote more than six hundred songs including dozens of hits for the Irving Berlin Music Company, but it was one afternoon at the Friars Club in New York City when he would pen a number that would truly stand the test of time. While waiting his turn at a billiard table, Donaldson began to think about his good fortune. He couldn't believe he was doing what he loved to do, spending times with people he enjoyed, living in what seemed like the creative center of the universe, and having a few dollars in his pocket. With those thoughts in mind, he sat down at a piano and created a tune that reflected good fortunes. A few days later, Donaldson gave lyricist George Whiting the new upbeat melody. Whiting quickly seized on the happy theme and completed "My Blue Heaven."

Donaldson and Whiting's song, which has been a hit for a number of artists in several different decades, reflects a spirit that many Christians need but lack. Often their eyes are so blinded by the world's flaws that they fail to realize that not only is heaven our destination after we die but also that we can claim a bit of it while we live.

When we accept Christ as our Savior, we should fear nothing. After all, how can anyone who is against us stack up to God? Paul, who was constantly being tormented by the establishment of his day, who had no home and few possessions, must have been smiling when he told his friends, "Hey, if I live, it gives me time to do even more work, but if I die, it is even better." In the midst of pain and suffering, Paul's faith had given him a bit of heaven on earth and look at how that affected his attitude!

In some cases, people's eyes are so focused on the next life that they simply fail to see how good they have it in this one. Waiting on heaven to fully appreciate God and God's blessings shows a lack of understanding and gratefulness for the Lord. God has given us people to love, a world to enjoy, work to do, and a way to help those who have less than we have. God has given us not only a place where we can claim happiness in our own blue heaven but also the power to give a taste of heaven to others as well.

So take your eyes off the ugliness in the world and

spend a few moments taking in the beauty that is everywhere. Go to a store and watch a child's eyes light up a toy display. Go to a park and look at young or even old lovers walking hand in hand down a path. Sit down in your favorite chair and contemplate how blessed you are to have food on the table, a roof over your head, and a place to call home while hundreds of millions in other places don't even have enough to eat. When you count your blessings as Paul did, you realize the life you've been given, even with all its problems and trials, is like having a bit of heaven on earth.

HOME SWEET HOME

But if it seems wrong in your opinion to serve the LORD, then choose today whom you will serve. Choose the gods whom your ancestors served beyond the Euphrates or the gods of the Amorites in whose land you live. But my family and I will serve the LORD. —Joshua 24:15

In *The Wizard of Oz* Dorothy exclaims, "There's no place like home." Men are fond of declaring, "A man's home is his castle!" At Christmas, radio stations play "There's No Place Like Home for The Holidays" and "I'll Be Home for Christmas". But maybe the best description of home is the statement, "Home is where the heart is," because a home reflects who we really are.

Certainly thoughts of the meaning of home have inspired everything from books to motion pictures, but perhaps the most beloved and well-known artistic rendering of home is the song "Home Sweet Home." The melody was provided by Sir Henry Bishop while the simple lyrics were penned by John Howard Payne and featured in his 1823 opera *Clari,*

Maid of Milan. The first lines, "Mid pleasures and palaces though we may roam, be it ever so humble, there's no place like home," still sum up the feelings of those who have fought in wars, served in faraway places, travelled on vacations or work, been away at school, or moved to find a new life. They are thoughts that likely hit home with the wealthy and the poor and young and old. Almost two centuries after it was penned, the song still speaks to people in every corner of the globe.

Two generations ago it was likely that most people would die no more than a few miles from where they were born. Some would live in the same home, and many would reside in the same communities their whole lives. But in the past fifty years, we have become a mobile world, and moving is not just an accepted part but an expected part of life. Thus, thoughts of having one "old home place" seem as antiquated as writing books on a typewriter. So the question becomes if you and your family cannot really go back to your ancestral house, then how can we define home in our modern age?

Thousands of years ago, Joshua declared that others could do as they wanted, but his house would always be one that embraced God. In our modern world, that means a great deal more than just owning a Bible, having a picture of Jesus on the wall, or even saying grace before a meal. Serving the Lord is defined by attitude, choice, love, and service. If we welcome others and share what we have, if we maintain Christian standards without judging, if we not only choose to read Jesus' words but also follow them, then our house has become a Christian home and the values learned there will go far beyond your home's walls. No matter where you live, no matter how many times you move, your home is where the heart is. If your heart is with the Lord, then your home will be a place, a very special and sweet place no matter how many times its address changes.

Smoke Gets in Your Eyes

*The god of this age has blinded the minds of those who don't
have faith so they couldn't see the light of the gospel that reveals
Christ's glory. Christ is the image of God.* —2 Corinthians 4:4

"Smoke Gets in Your Eyes" is a show tune written
by American composer Jerome Kern and lyricist Ott
Harback for their 1933 musical *Roberta*. It was performed in film by Irene Dunne and later recorded by
Paul Whiteman and His Orchestra, Nat "King" Cole,
Vic Damone, and a host of others. But perhaps the
most famous version of the now classic song was
recorded in 1958 by doo-wop legends—The Platters.
The lyrics speak of how love can blind folks to everything but the object of their affection. Thankfully,
while there are times love is anything but pre-
dictable; faith is much easier to figure out.

In the past two thousand years, hundreds of off-
shoots of the Christian faith have appeared. Many
disappeared just as quickly as they arrived on a scene,

but for at least a while, each new version of that old time religion made an impact and found people who were blinded by false promises and unproven viewpoints. Thousands of other non-Christian religions have also surfaced during this time, most claiming they had the latest and final answer in faith. In some cases, millions followed these new prophets' promises of a shortcut to happiness and fulfillment.

The lure of wealth, the drive for business, the power of money, the prosperity gospel, the draw of politics, and the promise made by the feel-good philosophies have all been successful in fogging over the lessons of faith to the point where people have been fooled into living for things that have no lasting value. In a sense, they sell their souls cheaply and never consider the consequences.

How do you prevent falling into the trap of straying from your faith? How do you know what to believe and what to dismiss? What to embrace and what to push away?

Consider what the world was like 2,000 years ago. Think about the way people lived during Jesus' time on earth. Compare and contrast the lifestyle of then and now. Go to the library and read about the often-barbaric rules that governed people's life. Move forward to American history. Consider the fact that it was not that long ago that slavery was legal and women couldn't vote. Try reading literature from eighty years ago. Almost everything you pick up and study will seem incredibly dated. Now go to your Bible.

Christ's words, found in the gospels, are as fresh and true today as they were 2,000 years ago. It is as if they could have been written for the information age. Jesus' parables have stood the test of time; they are applicable to each of us. After twenty centuries of unthinkable change, Christ is still not only relevant but also current. There is no need for an update, a reboot, or a new operating system. So when you start to get confused by the latest views on faith, all you need to do is reread Christ's words because they are a road map that stands the test of time.

$\mathcal{A}$ULD LANG SYNE

So then let's also run the race that is laid out in front of us, since we have such a great cloud of witnesses surrounding us. Let's throw off any extra baggage, get rid of the sin that trips us up, and fix our eyes on Jesus, faith's pioneer and perfecter. He endured the cross, ignoring the shame, for the sake of the joy that was laid out in front of him, and sat down at the right side of God's throne. —Hebrews 12:1-2

Beyond salvation, perhaps the greatest gift Christ gave His followers was the opportunity to wipe the slate clean and start all over. He allowed us to dump our baggage; He forgave us our past debts; He accepted us as we were and assured us that our new lives were going to better because He would be walking each step of the way with us. When you consider the unlimited scope of that gift, it is overwhelming. Maybe even more remarkable is that the gift of forgiveness is something we can begin with each day.

With this new life and a new road in front of us, how do we stay on track? The first step pointed out in Hebrews is to be surrounded by good influences. We need to learn from others who have more experience in this race and follow their examples.

The second step initially seems so very easy. We need to look to Jesus for guidance. But how is the best way to do that? Well, to know what Jesus would do, we must read the Bible and study His life. We must answer the questions of what do His parables mean to us? How can we live them out in our lives today? What was His attitude to those around Him? How did He treat those in need? Find those answers and we have our road map.

Finally, we must remember the price Jesus paid for us. We, therefore, must turn our eyes to the cross to see and feel what He endured.

If we can embrace those elements, then we can run our race with confidence and grace. In fact, starting our new life over will actually bring those around us a great deal of joy. To celebrate our new start, we might also want to sing an ancient song written by one of Scotland's greatest poets.

In 1788, Robert Burns penned new lyrics for a traditional folk song. In his "Auld Lang Syne," Burns wondered if old friends and good times needed to be remembered. In other words, should we look back or keep our eyes fixed on the future? For Christians, the answer is both. It is a tradition in Scotland to form a circle and join hands before singing "Auld Lang Syne". The song then unites instead of divides. In that way, it is a wonderful symbol of the inclusion that defines the Christian faith. Thus, as we move forward in our Christian lives, also let us follow this old custom by reaching out and including all races, backgrounds, and beliefs. There is no greater way to show you have been born again and are ready for the Christian road than by doing this simple act.

ONA LISA

You are utterly beautiful, my dearest; there's not a single flaw in you. —Song of Songs 4:7

In 1949, the Hall of Fame songwriting team of Ray Evans and Jay Livingston were commissioned to come up with a catchy musical number to feature in the film *Captain Carey, USA*. The composers pitched Paramount Studios an idea that used as its inspiration Leonardo da Vinci's painting *Mona Lisa*. The movie's producer and director loved the concept of a song about a mysterious woman being used in a spy film. It seemed a natural. Nelson Riddle and his orchestra were brought in to play the arrangement with Nat "King" Cole providing the vocals. While the song became a classic, the movie was quickly forgotten.

By today's standards, the woman who has come to be called Mona Lisa is not very striking. But a few hundred years ago, she must have been considered so beautiful that she earned a place as one of the world's greatest painter's models. Since then, she has inspired and enthralled countless millions of art lovers.

If da Vinci were looking for a model today, whom would you suggest that he choose? Is there someone you know who defines beauty? Is there someone in your life whose image could still fascinate people five centuries from now?

It has been said that life is a great deal like a beauty contest. Those who have looks and strength usually have a better chance of success in business, art, theater, film, and politics. Maybe that is true in the secular world, but in the Christian faith, how you look is not nearly as important as whom you reflect. If others see Jesus in you, then you are likely to be considered a beautiful person.

Though artists and motion pictures have influenced our image of Jesus, the Bible really doesn't give us a clue as to what He looked like. We don't know His height, weight, or the shape of His face. From a physical standpoint, we know almost nothing about Jesus. And perhaps that is best because it allows us to focus on what He said, how He lived, and what He had to teach us. It is the life of Jesus that is stunning. It is how He lived that defines beauty. It is His lessons in living that proclaim His Glory. No painting could fully capture those qualities.

ONA LISA

As the strains of "Mona Lisa" play in your head, rethink who are the most beautiful people in your life. Frame their images not in the way the world defines beauty but in the way they live. Are those you now think of as being beautiful people those who forgive easily, care deeply, and touch gently? Those whose hearts are full of grace are the people who are truly successful and beautiful. Maybe today you can have a complete makeover by doing nothing more that allowing others to see Jesus in you.

TENNESSEE WALTZ

I know the plans I have in mind for you, declares the LORD;
they are plans for peace, not disaster, to give you a future filled
with hope. —Jeremiah 29:11

In the 1940s, music groups usually travelled from concert to concert in cars. With five or six men and their instruments jammed into an auto, there was little room to move and very little to talk about. Pee Wee King's band was riding shoulder to shoulder across the south one long night when "Kentucky Waltz" came on the radio. Redd Stewart remarked, "Why does every state have a waltz song but Tennessee?" Pulling out a matchbook, Stewart began to jot down some lyrics, and as he read the lines out loud, the rest of the group invented a melody. By the time they'd made it home to Nashville, the song "Tennessee Waltz" had been born.

"Tennessee Waltz" is likely one of the saddest country ballads ever penned. The mournful theme centers on a broken heart that won't heal and a mind that forever looks back in regret. The lyrics tell of a waltz that will forever be tied to a love that got away. In 1950, Oklahoma-born Patti Page recorded the definitive version of Stewart's waltz. Her record was a monster hit and became the second-most-popular single of all time behind Bing Crosby's "White Christmas."

Few knew as much about loss and suffering as did Chicago businessman Horatio Spafford. In 1871, Spafford was looking forward to accompanying his family on a highly anticipated European vacation. Then a business problem threw a kink in his plans. Sensing he could take care of the issue fairly quickly, he sent his wife and four daughters on ahead. He assured them he would catch up them within a week of their arrival in France. Yet the children never made it. Even though their mother was saved, Spafford's daughters died when their ship went down in the Atlantic.

On his way to join his wife in Europe, the mourning man declared his faith in a song we still sing today, "It Is Well With My Soul." But he didn't stop there. Vowing to do something in his children's memory, Spafford and his wife moved to Palestine and, for many years, used their savings to feed hungry street orphans.

We cannot allow ourselves to live looking backwards at excruciating events in our past. No matter how great the pain, we must move forward. And if we truly have faith, then we can. After all, God promised us a future filled with hope. But like the lover who refuses to seek a new life and a new love, many fall into the trap of not letting go.

Tragedy will fall into almost all of our lives. But if we dwell on what has gone wrong in life, then we become victims. Like Horatio Spafford, we must have faith that God has a plan for our future. If we don't move forward, then we will spend our lives lost in the past and sadly dance alone.

WHEN YOU WISH UPON A STAR

The LORD is close to everyone who calls out to him, to all who call out to him sincerely. —Psalm 145:18

There is an ancient, simple Mother Goose rhyme that goes,

> Star light star bright,
> the first star I see tonight,
> I wish I may, I wish I might,
> have the wish I wish tonight.

This poem, combined with the ancient practice of wishing on stars, set the stage for the creation of what would become one of the Disney Corporation's theme songs. "When You Wish Upon a Star" was penned by Leigh Harline and Ned Washington for the 1940 movie adaption of the classic children's tale *Pinocchio*. Placing the song in the film made perfect sense as the animated feature starred a wooden puppet wishing to be a real, live boy.

The world of literature is alive with stories of men

who seek wishes. For generations, Christmas catalogs were called wish books. Before the candles are blown out on a birthday cake, people are encouraged to make a wish. In truth, maybe the biggest wishers of all are those who try to make it big in the world gambling or by buying a lottery ticket. In almost all the cases of wishing, the odds are against the wisher.

Paul explained the difference in being a mature and an immature Christian in 1 Corinthians 13, and it seemed to come down to simple motivation. Why did we want something, and what did we want to do with it? One passage in that Scripture is much deeper than it initially appears. To paraphrase the apostle in verse 11: When I was a child, my thoughts were shallow and without much depth, but as an adult, my thoughts are of a different and deeper nature. In other words, maturity brings understanding, and understanding teaches us the most important elements of life. But how does maturity change our wishes?

Pinocchio was more childlike than he realized. He embraced a characteristic of most immature people. He was innately selfish. Life was all about what he wanted. Thinking of others was simply not a part of his fiber. That was usually the case when each of us looked at Christmas wish books. We didn't search the pages to find special gifts for others; we carefully sought out the things we wanted. But how did our parents use those same catalogs? They sought gifts for others not themselves.

Christian life is not about selfish wishing—it is about unselfish giving. Thus we must not spend our hours wishing on stars or searching for a shortcut to fortune. That is not just a waste of our time but a waste of God's gifts as well. Instead we need to focus on the world around us, seeking out the needs of our family, friends, and those less fortunate, and then pray (rather than wish) for a way we can meet those needs. When we make that thinking a natural part of lives, we move past childish wishes and into a world of fulfillment, a world never found by those who only wish and never pray. That world is filled with purpose, joy, and love.

$\mathcal{S}$ECRET LOVE

Jesus spoke to the people again, saying, "I am the light of the world. Whoever follows me won't walk in darkness but will have the light of life." —John 8:12

In 1953, Sammy Fain and Paul Francis Webster were given the task of composing music for a Doris Day film based on the life of the western legend Calamity Jane. While the script was largely fictional, the movie proved one of the most popular of the year with Fain and Webster's ballad "Secret Love" becoming one of the top hits of the decade.

In a sense, secret loves are very sad. A love that can't be made public is a product of several different things. The most obvious is shyness. Many people simply can't come to admit their love because they fear it being rejected. Another reason for a secret love might well be the fear of commitment. Many question if they have what it takes to fully dedicate themselves to another human being. A third reason loves remain secret is due to dishonesty. Sadly many secret loves involve adultery. A final reason for secret love is a sense of unworthiness. Many simply lack the confidence to believe they measure up.

The Doris Day hit single begins as a sad story but ends triumphantly as she overcomes all of her misgivings about hiding her true emotions. When she made the courageous step to reveal how she felt, it was rewarded by her finding the love of a lifetime. Thus, she was able to shout out her story to the whole world!

A lot of Christians seem to have a secret love when it comes to matters of faith. They are so scared that their friends or associates might condemn or mock them for their beliefs; they refuse to show their Christian love in public. So while they have accepted Christ, they have kept Him as a secret Savior.

There was once a time when this secret faith might have been natural. Early Christians were often executed or tossed to hungry lions. In England, Catholics were once drawn and quartered for sharing their faith even within their own families. Yet what stops us now? When was the last time a person you knew was arrested for going to church or giving his or her testimony? When was the last time someone was sent to the gallows for reading a Bible on a New York park bench? In truth, in our free society, there is nothing to fear about declaring our love for Christ. So why do so many professed Christians never display that love in public? Just like many whose hearts are fixed on another human heart, they are either shy, fear rejection, or lack commitment.

Keeping your faith hidden will not bar you from heaven, but it might close the door for someone else. Jesus saved you not just to secure an afterlife; He infused us with light to share His story with the world now. If we are truly proud to follow Him, if we believe He is who the Bible says He is, then we need to proclaim it in the way we live. That doesn't mean we have to shout it from the highest hill, but it does call for us not to be afraid to share our faith or reflect Jesus in the way we treat and love others.

Don't Be Cruel

Hate stirs up conflict, but love covers all offenses.

—*Proverbs 10:12*

In 1956, Elvis Presley's incredible rise to the top of the entertainment world was in full swing. From out of nowhere, the kid from Memphis had become the biggest star in show business. Thus, every songwriter on the planet was trying to land the next Presley single.

On Christmas Eve, 1955, a former dry cleaner employee turned tunesmith, Otis Blackwell, talked himself into a job with Shalimar Music in New York City and immediately began supplying the company with fresh, creative material. But while being recorded by minor acts—recording his music sure beat pressing pants—Blackwell needed a real hit to feel secure and shake the bill collectors from his tail. Thus he listened to Presley's music to get a feel for what the singer liked. Blackwell then studied the kids who were buying Elvis's music to find out what they were interested in. What the writer discovered was that teens lived every day like it was their last, and thus, each new emotion lifted them into the clouds or plunged them deep into the valleys. Combining the style Presley liked with a teen's emotional rollercoaster lifestyle, Blackwell wrote "Don't Be Cruel." The single would become the biggest seller in the Elvis catalog.

On the surface, the song, about a guy who is begging the girl he has a crush on to be nice, seems like little more than fluff. Yet, a second look reveals something a bit deeper. This is a song about devotion and respect. The young man is willing to give his heart to the girl, but he needs her to at least treat him as if he has some value.

We live in a world where hate seems to be everywhere, and understanding and acceptance are often in short supply and hard to find. Flip on talk radio and some cable TV outlets and you'll find commentators and hosts who use hate to stir up conflict. Sadly, some who listen and live on a steady diet of this type of entertainment withdraw from a world they see as having no place for them. Contrast this to Jesus's way of communication.

When Jewish religious leaders of Christ's day disparaged Samaritans, Jesus turned them into heroes.

He also opened His heart to prostitutes, lepers, and those weak of spirit. I feel, even at their first meeting, that the sinners around Jesus must have viewed him as a friend. That friendship, brought on by not condemning folks, opened the door for Christ to give people a sense of real value, and that led to dramatic and positive change.

As it says in Proverbs, love covers all offenses. It opens doors, it is forgiving, and it leads people back to where they need to be. Look at what Christ accomplished just by loving even those who deserved it the least. So maybe by remembering Elvis's biggest hit from 1956, we can truly be a person who reacts the way Christ would and reflects Him in all our relationships. The first step might be as simple as never being cruel.

I'm So Lonesome I Could Cry

God created humanity in God's own image, in the divine image God created them, male and female God created them.
—Genesis 1:27

Some have called Hank Williams' "I'm So Lonesome I Could Cry" the saddest song ever composed. This number, written not long after Hank and his wife had broken up, presents a stark view of a man's great loneliness. In mournful lyrics, you can almost feel Williams' depression and pain.

When God saw Adam was lonely, something new was added to the garden of Eden. Yet there are many relationships where people live in the same house but are alone. The reason is a lack of communication. If you don't visit with your spouse, if you don't find out what is happening in his or her life and share what is going on in yours, if you fail to reveal problems or celebrate joys, then it easy to feel as if you are walking through the world all by yourself. Well, the same thing is true with God.

If we have a living relationship with the Lord and talk daily in prayer, then we will likely rarely feel completely alone. Sadly Hank Williams likely didn't realize this when he penned the lyrics to "I'm So Lonesome I Could Cry." Many today feel like Hank. They are the people who call the suicide hot lines, get lost in drugs or alcohol, or who cry themselves to sleep each night. They are the folks who hang onto hope by one thin thread. Not only do they not have friends in their lives, but they also can't seem to connect with God.

There are many ways to find the lonely in your world, but to do so requires two very important things. The first is a caring heart. You have to want to seek out those in pain and comfort them. The most common excuse given for not doing this is "I don't know what to say." What you say is not nearly as important as being there. The fact is most lonely people have a deep need to talk; therefore, your job will likely be just to listen.

The other element you must have is vision. Christ had an eye for seeing the needy and hurting that others missed. There are lonely people on your church rolls, and your pastor can direct you to them. There are isolated souls in nursing homes. Your mailman or policeman likely knows of lonely people as well. These solitary souls need to realize that no matter their situation that God still cares for them. You might be the only person who will bring them that news.

If you are lonely and feel as if "I'm So Lonesome I Could Cry" could be your theme song, then seek out help. There are pastors who want to help you. Don't be afraid to meet with them. But if your life is in order, then find a few minutes to find someone who needs a friend. That simple act might be the most important thing you will ever do. There is nothing like bringing sunshine to a person who has been living in a dark world.

$\mathscr{B}$RIDGE OVER TROUBLED WATERS

There is one God and one mediator between God and human-ity, the human Christ Jesus. —1 Timothy 2:5

Simon and Garfunkel were once one of the hottest duos in entertainment. In 1966, they scored their first major hit with "Sounds of Silence." Their folk harmonies are still rocking the world four decades later.

In 1969, Art Garfunkel took a break from touring to try his hand at acting. While he was in Hollywood, Paul Simon opted to come up with new material for the pair's next recording session. When creating what would become the duo's biggest hit, Simon pulled from an obscure band known as the Swan Silvertones and a line from their song "Mary Don't You Weep." Recycling the phrase, "I'll be your bridge over troubled waters if you trust me," would make history.

"Bridge Over Troubled Waters" was a song with a message so simple and timeless that it has spoken to three generations and will likely touch a dozen more. When people are in a quandary, when they have problems and see no way out, they pray that someone will appear and lead them beyond the heartache, pain, and hopelessness to a world that offers a chance at new life. For Christians, faith is the bridge, and Jesus is the one who built it and is there to guide from one side to the other. Scores of folks around us right now have no faith and no hope, and therefore, there is no bridge.

Consider the plight of the lepers during Christ's walk on earth. They were reviled, shunned, and cursed. They were not only in great pain but also in fear of wasting away before their eyes. They were not allowed to work or participate in society. Even religious leaders avoided them and told these poor people that it was their sins that created their condition. For them, there was no bridge from their sad and hopeless world to the place where everyone else lived. Then Jesus stepped into their lives.

Today we often focus on Jesus cleansing the lepers as just another miracle. We see the act as spectators rather than participants. In the shock and awe of this healing, we fail to consider what the lepers must have felt. Imagine an entire world has been once more opened up to you. There are no limits or shame.

Imagine once more being accepted. Try to compre-hend what an overwhelming gift that must have been.

While Christ saved us through grace, He also used grace to build bridges from hopelessness to hope for those He met in the world. And that should be our charge as well. We need to seek out those whose troubles are too large for them to handle all by them-selves and help them find a way to a better place. For some, that might come through spiritual guidance or a simple prayer, for others some kind of physical aid. For a child or young person, it might mean that we become mentors. But if we are to be like Christ, then we must be that bridge for those who are drowning in those troubled waters.

$\mathscr{I}$'LL BE THERE

*For where two or three are gathered in my name, I'm there with
them. —Matthew 18:20*

It is rare to find a pop hit that was inspired by a
passage from the New Testament, but that is just
what happened in 1970 when the Jackson Five took
"I'll Be There" to the top of the American charts. The
story behind the number might be one of the most
interesting to come out of the Detroit music scene.
Motown CEO Berry Gordy assigned Hal Davis,
Willie Hutch, and Bob West to come up with a
change of pace song for the Jacksons, who were at
that time considered a bubblegum soul group. Gordy
wanted something serious for the five brothers to
record—a ballad with a message.

As they considered a theme for their collaborative
work, the songwriters pulled their inspiration from
Matthew 18:20. In this simple verse, Jesus assures His
followers that even when just a few of them are gathered, He will also be there with them. While using

this comforting thought as a starting point, the trio shifted the message to one where a man assures a woman he will be there for her no matter what she needs. He further states that his love will remain true even if she chooses someone else. In a sense, "I'll Be There" represents love and friendship that was so forgiving that it knew no bounds.

As Christians, we are called to be Christ on earth. We therefore need to follow His lead in everything we do. That means that just like He assured everyone who knew Him that He would always be there when they gathered or were in need, so should we. That doesn't mean that we can always be with our friends; sometimes that is simply impossible, but they need to know that, when times are tough, they can count on our support and love. Yet that is just the beginning. We must go a step further than simply "being there" in order to truly emulate Jesus.

Humans have a nature to be exclusive rather than inclusive. This often even carries over into how they worship. We each have a tendency to bond with those who are just like us and stay away from others who don't live up to our standards. Well, as no one has ever lived up to Christ's standards, if He had followed this course, then He would have associated with no one. Jesus put no conditions on those who called His name. He did not demand they be perfect. He accepted their faults and forgave them of their sins. We must do the same. It is just as important for us to be there for those who don't share our faith, standards, or morals as it was for Christ to be there for them. We also need to give freely to those who have hurt us. And that takes forgiveness. For a Christian, that giving and forgiving spirit should be as natural as breathing.

Who is hurting around you today? Who needs a friend? Who do you need to forgive? Today might be the time to assure that you will be there!

$\mathscr{I}$ Can't Stop Loving You

Jesus replied, "The most important one is Israel, listen! Our God is the one Lord, and you must love the Lord your God with all your heart, with all your being, with all your mind, and with all your strength." —Mark 12:29-30

In 1955, a struggling country music singer/songwriter was sitting by himself in a small, mobile home just outside of Knoxville, Tennessee. Don Gibson was just another one of thousands attempting to find something that would put his career on the map. Needing a hit, he picked up a pencil, piece of paper, and his guitar and worked to come up with anything original that would stand out from the words of other songwriters of the era. His sense of loneliness became his inspiration. Putting himself into a position of loving someone who didn't return that love, he came up with what would be one of his first hits and, over time, one of the most recorded songs in the history of country music.

Gibson's "I Can't Stop Loving You" followed the release of "Oh Lonesome Me," ironically another song composed on that lonely day in the mobile home. Those two songs launched a career that lasted decades and put Gibson into the Country Music Hall of Fame.

The apostle Paul just might have liked the title to this hit country song. Except, if Paul had written it, he would have probably flipped the lyrics. The missionary's song would have centered on the story of a man who constantly moved forward because of a Savior whom he couldn't stop loving. After all, Paul was the one who wrote in 1 Corinthians that love was greater than all other things. And the love of which the missionary wrote was that which came from God.

Open any hymnal in any church and you will soon be overwhelmed by the volume of songs that have been composed with love as the theme. Look deeper into the lyrics and you will see time and time again the story of God's love for man. "Oh how I love Jesus, because He first loved me," "Jesus loves me this I know," and "Jesus loves the little children" are just a few of the lines that bring meaning and hope to the songs of praise that are sung each week. Each of them reflects on something that even many

Christians forget. God made the first step. We didn't have to climb a high mountain or build a huge cathedral to find Him. He was there all the time. His love costs us nothing. He will not turn His back on us no matter what we do. In fact, He loves us even when we don't acknowledge Him.

Most parents love their children no matter what they do. They might be disappointed and hurt by their kids' actions, but they forgive them for their wrongs and never stop loving them. God's ability to forgive and love is ever greater than that of the world's best parent. He has assured us that He loved us even before we were born and would never stop loving us no matter our course in life. Yes, "He Can't Stop Loving You," and that is something to be thankful for and sing about!

Can't Buy Me Love

But the fruit of the Spirit is love, joy, peace, patience, kindness, goodness, faithfulness, gentleness, and self-control. There is no law against things like this. —Galatians 5:22-23

In the midst of The Beatles' incredible rise to fame and fortune, Paul McCartney realized that he could literally buy anything he could imagine. It was a sobering thought. If he wanted a diamond ring, then he could just buy it. There was no car or home he couldn't afford. For him, a shopping spree could go on for years. This should have made him the happiest man in the world, but instead it left him feeling a bit hollow. He would later say of the song that was inspired by that moment: "The idea behind it was that all these material possessions are all very well, but they won't buy me what I really want." McCartney was in Paris staying at one of the world's most expensive hotels when he sat down at a piano and wrote about something that he had come to realize money couldn't buy, and that was love.

Love has been written about more than any other subject in world history. Love has been the quest of those who have everything as well as those who have nothing. Fortunes have been lost in chasing love, and love has been lost in chasing fortunes. But in more than six thousand years of recorded history, man has yet to find a way to actually purchase this one commodity that he most needs and wants.

Love also has another unique quality. It is the one thing that can be given away without the giver losing it. In fact, a person who truly offers love to another is blessed with even more love in his or her life. That in itself defies logic. But then love rarely comes to a logical mind.

It has been written that God is love. The New Testament echoes this throughout its pages. Love is why Jesus died. Love in the most important gift. Love causes us to mature and give up selfish things.

In human relationships, to be loved, you first must give love. But in God's world, love is offered even when we do not follow Him or keep His commandments. Thus while love might be the most elusive thing to find in the human world, it is only a prayer away in the Christian world.

Yet that is the just the beginning. As it says in Galatians, love is a fruit of the spirit. That makes it a gift, and gifts need to be shared with others. It only takes a spark to get a fire started, and it only takes you showing love to soften a hardened heart, reach a lonely person, or heal a hurting spirit.

The thing that money can't buy God has given to you. Take it and run with it. Show that love in the way you speak to others. Use it to lift spirits. Give it to others, and it will come back to you in ways you cannot begin to imagine. Giving love freely defines your mature faith and your complete understanding of why Jesus died for you.

RAINDROPS KEEP FALLIN' ON MY HEAD

The LORD is close to the brokenhearted; he saves those whose spirits are crushed. —Psalm 34:18

"Into each life a bit of rain must fall." What that ancient proverb points out is that everyone will experience a bit of heartache and pain. In this imperfect world it can't be avoided.

Nancy Muirhead was a young woman who fully understood this. Cancer first struck her when she was just out of college. A few years later, just as she and her husband were about to adopt a child, cancer again came back into the elementary school teacher's life. She was thirty-two when it hit her the third time. I had known Nancy since college. She was a vibrant, beautiful, energetic woman who spoke about one hundred fifty words a minute with gusts up to two twenty-five. She loved life and relished every new experience. She feared nothing and had faith as deep as the ocean. When I asked her if she ever looked at her cancer and asked, "Why me?" her response was quick and direct: "No, I say why not me. I have faith, and I can handle this. Besides, I would rather take this on than have it strike someone I know and love." What a wise perspective!

Nancy lived only thirty-three years, and during that time, she didn't dwell on misfortune but instead embraced the challenges it brought. She never felt sorry for herself either; therefore, where others saw rain, she seemed to always find rainbows.

In 1968, Hal David and Burt Bacharach allowed their latest composition to be used in the Hollywood western/comedy *Butch Cassidy and the Sundance Kid*. B. J. Thomas cut "Raindrops Keeps Fallin' on My Head" in eight takes. The single hit #1 on the charts and earned the Academy Award for Best Original Song.

"Raindrops Keeps Fallin' on My Head" presents the attitude Nancy embraced each day of her life. She was not going to dwell on the rain but, instead, was going to search the clouds for the rainbows. She adopted this attitude because she was sure God would carry her on their days she couldn't carry herself.

The next time a problem falls into your world, consider Nancy's viewpoint. Would you rather have this issue visit someone you loved? Would you rather he or she have to confront it? If we truly have a Christ-like attitude, then the answer is obvious. We want to take on the problems of life rather than have some-one we love experience them.

The clouds will gather, and the rain will fall. As we deal with those storms, others will look our way to see how we react. If we moan and complain, if we shake our fists and yell out "this isn't fair," then we might have company in our misery, but we will feel no better and will have inspired no one. God didn't promise us a pain-free life, but He did assure us that He would be there with us in that pain. Nancy no doubt saw the theme found in "Raindrops Keep Fallin' on My Head" as the attitude to embrace in the darkest days of her Christian walk. What about you?

ℬATTLE HYMN OF THE REPUBLIC

So then, if anyone is in Christ, that person is part of the new creation. The old things have gone away, and look, new things have arrived! —2 Corinthians 5:17

In 1861, during the early days of the Civil War, writer/publisher Julia Ward Howe rode with her husband and two other men in a carriage through the streets of Washington D.C. As they made the slow trip across town, they observed on almost every street corner soldiers singing, "John Brown's body lies a-mouldering in the grave." After hearing it for the sixth time, Dr. James Clark, a minister, turned to Massachusetts Governor John Andrews and the Howes and casually noted, "It is a shame such a wonderful melody has been used with those depressing lyrics." His observation made such a mighty impact that that night, in a hotel room, unable to sleep, Julia rose from bed and sat at a table. She later described the experience: "This soul-inspiring song was the incarnation of patriotic and martial feeling. It was struck out of the white heat of unconscious inspiration, the soul's product of a mighty movement." Driven by the voice she couldn't hear, Howe scribbled out a poem meant to be married to the tune of "John Brown's Body."

Howe reworded the lyrics several times before giving them to *The Atlantic Journal*. The magazine printed her "Mine Eyes Have Seen the Glory" in early 1862. Within a year, the anthem was so popular across the Union states that it was employed as a rallying cry for the war effort. Abraham Lincoln called it the most uplifting composition he had ever heard.

Just like few others saw the potential in the song "John Brown's Body," many in Jesus' time had problems understanding the second birth. They missed the mark because they related to the physical rather than the spiritual. Even today, that element of Christianity is often hard for many to fully comprehend. But by using "Battle Hymn of the Republic" as a platform, it becomes very easy to explain the difference between a life without Christ and one with him as Lord.

Just as Howe's new lyrics transformed a depressing song of death into an anthem of faith, hope, and life, so you can be changed as well. No matter how far you have slipped, no matter what you have done, and no matter how deep your sins, you can be remade. That makeover won't change your outward appearance, but it will dramatically alter your spiritual outlook and direction.

Each life is a song, and initially, the verses are mournful because the ending of the story is sure to be death. Therefore, as life seems to have no reason or purpose, depression and sadness often hang over lost souls like the clouds of war. But Christ conquered death and gave real purpose to life. He therefore wrote new lyrics to life's song that include hope, love, and peace. A Christ-filled life also means service. Understanding that final element of our song of life allows us to fully adopt Julia Ward Howe's incredible words as our own. "As He died to make men holy let us live to make men free." It is time to get marching!

You're a Grand Ole Flag

The Lord replied, "If you had faith the size of a mustard seed, you could say to this mulberry tree, 'Be uprooted and planted in the sea,' and it would obey you. —Luke 17:6

In 1905, stage star, songwriter, and producer George M. Cohan was driving to New York City when he saw an elderly man, shabbily dressed, walking along the side of the road. Cohan sensed the poor man could use a lift and possibly a few dollars, so the toast of Broadway stopped his open roadster and called back to the refugee from the previous century. The scruffy man eyed the car suspiciously before wearily climbing in. As Cohan shifted his horseless carriage back into gear, he noticed his passenger was carefully cradling some fabric in his arms. Sensing its importance, the producer asked about it.

In a weakened voice, the man explained he had been a flag bearer at the Battle of Gettysburg. He was serving with the Union forces the day of Pickett's charge.

His horse had been shot out from under him, but the veteran proudly declared, "The flag never hit the ground. I never dropped it." It was then Cohan realized the rag the man was holding was the flag he had been carrying more than fifty years before. Later that day, inspired by that moment, the Broadway producer penned what would become one of America's best-loved patriotic anthems, "You're a Grand Ole Flag".

So many Christians take great pride in waving the Stars and Stripes. They celebrate each holiday by parading this symbol out and proudly using it to declare their loyalty to the United States. This patriotism is to be applauded, but we also need to remember to proudly carry the banner of Christ.

"Onward Christian Soldiers" is often thought of as the theme song for the Salvation Army, but the song predates the organization. It was written by an Anglican priest in England for a children's church parade. The hymn's message was to proudly show your faith as you marched for Jesus.

The old Civil War veteran took his duties to protect the flag very seriously. Long after the war ended and he entered civilian life, the symbol he had fought for stayed with him. How seriously do we carry the banner of Christ in our lives? Can people see Jesus so clearly in our actions that they stop and ask us about our faith? Is it as easy for us to talk about Christ as it is to trumpet our love for our country?

It seems likely the old vet felt the most important moment of his life was the time he didn't drop the flag. It appears that he never moved forward after that moment. Sadly, many Christians never move past John 3:16. They accept Christ as their Savior but never show it in their actions or by displaying a loving spirit. Just like the old man, they celebrate a moment but don't use that moment to build a new life. Faith needs to be shown, not hidden. It needs to be such a natural part of our lives that people are drawn to ask us why we are different. Faith put into action is the way we declare our love for Christ and our understanding of His mission. That faith is never old, just grand!

$\mathscr{M}$Y WAY

*Although I'm free from all people, I make myself a slave to all
people, to recruit more of them. I act like a Jew to the Jews,
so I can recruit Jews. I act like I'm under the Law to those
under the Law, so I can recruit those who are under the Law
(though I myself am not under the Law). I act like I'm outside
the Law to those who are outside the Law, so I can recruit
those outside the Law (though I'm not outside the law of God
but rather under the law of Christ). I act weak to the weak, so
I can recruit the weak. I have become all things to all people,
so I could save some by all possible means. All the things I do
are for the sake of the gospel, so I can be a partner with it.*
—*1 Corinthians 9:19-23*

In 1969, former teen idol and songwriter Paul
Anka had dinner with Frank Sinatra. As the meal
progressed, it became obvious Sinatra was frustrated
by the way musical tastes had evolved. He even
spoke about quitting the business. After returning
home, Anka reviewed Frank's remarkable career and
was inspired to create a song called "My Way."

Anka's effort would generate a new hit for Sinatra and become one of the most recorded numbers in music history. Yet while the composition accurately describes the path Sinatra's life took, a short look at the life of an apostle points out that this likely shouldn't be our theme song.

When Paul was Saul, he did things his way. He charted his course, made his own rules, and served as judge and jury. When Christ came into Saul's life, the man made a dramatic change in the way he lived. No longer was his theme song "My Way," instead it became "His Way"! He found that giving up control didn't weaken him but brought him great strength.

We need to reexamine the focus in our lives. Is it on us or on God? Are we living each day representing Jesus in our thoughts and actions, or are we doing things our own way? Do the standards we set, the reactions we have, and the goals we meet reflect us rather than the Lord?

Just as Paul Anka used Frank Sinatra's life to create the song "My Way," it might be good to put your life on paper too. Jot down your accomplishments, the most important things in your life, the people who are your greatest influences, those you have helped and the reasons you came to their aid, and your goals for the next few years. Once you have those in front of you, make a check mark beside the elements of your life that were done your way and a star beside those that were done God's way. Who wins in your life? You or God?

When Paul was dying, he could look back at two lives. In the first one, he did things his own way and reflected all the shortcomings of man. But in the second life, he was God's man and everything Paul did was for the Lord. Therefore, whereas Saul had many regrets, Paul had none.

$\mathscr{L}$ET IT BE

"Peace I leave with you. My peace I give you. I give to you not as the world gives. Don't be troubled or afraid. You have heard me tell you, 'I'm going away and returning to you.' If you loved me, you would be happy that I am going to the Father, because the Father is greater than me. I have told you before it happens so that when it happens you will believe. I won't say much more to you because this world's ruler is coming. He has nothing on me. Rather, he comes so that the world will know that I love the Father and do just as the Father has commanded me. Get up. We're leaving this place." —John 14:27-31

By 1969, it was obvious that the world's most famous rock band was in a state of flux. Word from both the inside and the outside was that The Beatles were on the verge of breaking up. Their sound was changing, and the groups' members were not in agreement as to the direction this musical evolution needed to go. Paul McCartney was deeply troubled by the infighting he was seeing in the group. Ironically, that created the environment for a song that would become a fitting way for the quartet to say good-bye to their fans.

McCartney's mother died when he was just fourteen. Though the woman made a long and courageous fight against cancer, it was the disease that claimed victory. Thus Mary never got to see her son graduate from school, much less rise to the top of the entertainment world and become almost as recognized a symbol for England as the Union Jack. Just when it became apparent The Beatles were going to dissolve, McCartney had a dream where he was reintroduced his mother. Just before he woke up, Mary assured him, "It will be all right, just let it be."

Humans are limited in our control. Simply put, there are things we can't change. Songwriters, such as Paul McCartney, have a ready avenue to examine their frustrations. They just pull out pen and paper and put their thoughts into verse. But what do we do when unmanageable situations confront us? I have a friend who simply writes his problem on a slip of paper, pulls out a Mason jar, and drops the note in. After he reseals the lid, he pauses, says a prayer, and moves on. This is his way of letting go and letting God.

When she was alive, McCartney's mother, Mary, had likely told her son scores of times, "It will be all right, just let it be." That is why those words came to him during his time of need. And that is not just sound advice; it is Biblical. Jesus encouraged us to do the same while telling us not to worry, "God is in control." Accepting and admitting our weakness is often a challenge, but it also opens the door for new opportunities. As it says in John 14:31, it is time to get moving. Put what you can't change out of your mind and step forward in faith realizing there is something better ahead. We can't know what that something is, but unless we let what we can't change just be, we will never find out.

Can't Help Falling in Love with You

The person who doesn't love does not know God, because God is love. —1 John 4:8

In 1960, George David Weiss was one of the most recognized and honored songwriters in the world. He had spun hits on Broadway, in the motion picture industry, and for a plethora of music icons. It was therefore natural that Paramount Pictures would approach Weiss about providing music for the company's newest film *Hawaiian Beach Boy*. Weiss read through the script and recognized a spot for a tender ballad. He took this new song to the producers who were not impressed. Though a demo was cut, no one planned to share the song with the film's star. Nevertheless, Elvis Presley heard the record as he walked by an office, stopped, and told the executives he really liked it. When Presley was informed that the silly little song wasn't right for the film, he stood his ground. In the end, the singer's love for Weiss's ballad paved the way for "Can't Help Falling in Love with You" to become the highlight of the film, now renamed *Blue Hawaii*, and one of the most beloved Elvis songs in history.

Just as Presley's love of the song paved the way for it to find a place in the hearts of millions, God's love for us paves the way for incredible opportunities. First of all, it saves us from our sins. That is a pretty large gift all by itself. But, if His love shines through us, then that love also opens the door to doing so much more.

As a boy, Albert Schweitzer spent hours staring at the stature of a man literally holding the weight of the world on his shoulders. What was most profound to Schweitzer was an African was lifting this massive burden. Yet, as the boy studied history, he understood that men from Europe and America who had called themselves Christians had enslaved millions of these same Africans as well as plundered the riches from their lands. As Schweitzer grew older and surrendered to call to the ministry, he asked congregations, "Where have we shown the love of Christ to Africa?"

In order to right a wrong, Schweitzer would go to medical school and then leave the comforts of his home in Europe and move to the jungles of Africa.

Tens of thousands of Christians had come to this land before him without showing the love of Christ and the missionary was determined to change that. Over the course of six decades, Schweitzer became the symbol of love for millions. And it all started with a statue and a young boy wondering how to best show God's love.

Right now, all around us, there are people wanting to know why loving Christians are not there to help them carry their burdens. Just like it took one man to discover Weiss's ballad and bring it to the world and one medical doctor to change the image of Europeans and Americans in Africa, you might be the one person who can help a troubled soul on this day discover Christ's love. God couldn't help loving you, but do you love Him enough to love the ones others overlook?

ʃ BELIEVE

*Jesus responded, "I assure you that if you have faith and don't
doubt, you will not only do what was done to the fig tree. You
will even say to this mountain, 'Be lifted up and thrown into
the lake.' And it will happen. If you have faith, you will receive
whatever you pray for." —Matthew 21:21-22*

Jane Froman was one of America's most popular
singers during World War II. She didn't sit the war
out either; she worked and travelled tirelessly for
the USO. She was in Europe entertaining Allied
troops in February 1943 when her plane crashed.
It would take thirty-nine operations just to fix one
of her legs well enough to be fitted with brace.
Within a year, the undaunted and heroic Froman
was on crutches and back in Europe once more
singing for GIs. When the war ended, her biggest
fans came home, and by the early 1950s, they
helped make Froman one of America's most popular television stars. But once more, the woman's
thoughts were not on her success but on the plight

of thousands of young men being called to another war.

The Korean conflict flooded Froman's mind with a host of memories. She couldn't believe the pain and suffering was happening all over again. As she read news of injuries and deaths, she was revisited by nightmares of men she'd seen maimed and dying in hospitals across Europe. Wanting to find a way to display her faith and assure those in her audience and fighting in Korea there was a God who loved them and cared for them, she asked Ervin Drake, Irvin Graham, Jimmy Shirl, and Al Stillman to compose a song echoing her beliefs. It took a bit of time, but the quartet of writers finally gave the singer what she wanted. "I Believe" was introduced on Froman's program in 1953 and became not just a hit song but also a national prayer.

Jesus assured us that faith was a tool far more powerful than even war. He told His followers that if they really believed, then they could move a mountain. And by all indications, moving a mountain was just the beginning. A person with enough faith could change the world. Although Froman's hit song didn't instantly bring peace to Korea, it did remind many that real peace could be found in another way.

Jane Froman's life indicated she understood faith

better than most. When she found great success, she used it to enrich others. She constantly gave back more than she was given. She pushed herself to do things few others would. In fact, when she retired from show business and returned to her hometown in Missouri, she saw it as a promotion to more important work. Until the day she died, her hands-on volunteer efforts in Columbia defined her much more than her long list of hit records.

Where are your prayers focused? Are you praying for a life that can be a blessing to others? Does your faith reflect your motives as well as your happiness? If you truly believe, then you will look outward rather than inward, see those who you can help rather than seek help, and use your success to lift others up and give them hope! But first you've got to believe to make things happen in both small and big ways!

$\mathcal{G}$OD ONLY KNOWS

Even if our hearts condemn us, God is greater than our hearts and knows all things. —1 John 3:20

As the front man for the rock group the Lovin' Spoonful, John Sebastian was already a well-known name with a long list of chart topping hits when he sat down to write a song with the Beach Boy's Brian Wilson. On the surface, the two men, one from New York City and the other from California, couldn't have been more different. Sebastian embraced a folk style that seemed to have little in common with Wilson's eclectic mix of classical and surf music. So it was not surprising that Wilson almost called the whole thing off because Sebastian wouldn't change the song's opening line, "I may not always love you." Wilson thought it was far too negative. When they finally opted to keep the first line, another issue reared its head. The last hit song with God in the title had been three decades before when Kate Smith had scored with "God Bless America." Even after "God

Only Knows" was recorded and those in the studio were calling it the best Beach Boy record ever, Wilson had doubts about the public's acceptance of a song he saw as being very spiritual and religious.

"God Only Knows" was released in the United States as a B side. While in the United States radio stations played "Wouldn't It Be Nice," in the United Kingdom disc jockeys went with "God Only Knows." Thus the song that was supposed to be ignored became a worldwide hit single for America's best-known band. Over the next three decades, "God Only Knows" was cut by a wide variety of artists, and the Beach Boys' original version has been chosen as one of the top twenty greatest songs of the rock and roll era.

To those in the music business, it now seems silly that a song that mentioned God and spoke of love that lasts forever was almost thrown away. With its complex theme but simple lyrics and magical arrangement, it seemed to have hit written all over it. So why was Brian Wilson so apprehensive about releasing it? Perhaps it was for the same reason we have trouble speaking publicly about faith.

It is pretty easy for most of us to talk about how much the Lord means to us when we are in church. We have no problem singing the great old hymns or asking someone to pray for us in a sanctuary. But stepping out those doors and into the real world quoting Scripture or humming "Amazing Grace" or "Victory in Jesus" often makes us uncomfortable. Why do we hesitate to speak in public the way we speak in church? It is probably for the same reason Brian Wilson toyed with changing the title of "God Only Knows"; we are afraid of what people will think.

How many "hits" have we missed in life thanks to our fears? In this case, hits are chances to share our faith with others. If you think it, then have the boldness to say it. That is the difference in being a confident Christian who looks for opportunities to use God's name and one that is lukewarm and runs from saying God in public.

Here Comes the Sun

Don't look to the skies, to the sun or the moon or the stars, all the heavenly bodies, and be led astray, worshipping and serving them. The LORD your God has granted these things to all the nations who live under heaven. —Deuteronomy 4:19

By 1969, George Harrison had pretty much come to the conclusion that being famous and wealthy was often much more trouble that it was worth. He was trapped by his notoriety and could not make a move in public without being constantly hounded by the press and fans. The one thing he loved to do, make music, was now compromised by the size, scope, and demands of The Beatles' business worldwide empire. He was expected to be in the office every day, keeping regular hours studying new deals, working with clients, reading contracts, and meeting with employees. As he gave more and more of himself to his career, he longed for days without demands that were filled with sunshine rather than cold rain and gray skies. One afternoon, when he had all he could stand, Harrison played hooky and went to visit his friend Eric Clapton. As luck would have it, the sun came out and the temperatures warmed enough for Harrison to take a guitar outside and walk around the garden. Forgetting about his demands and obligations, he again felt like a carefree child. And with that fresh viewpoint, he was inspired to write "Here Comes the Sun." The next day, as he shared his new composition with his staff, his office duties didn't seem nearly as foreboding.

Many of us can identify with George Harrison. While we may not be dealing with fame or fortune, things are constantly pulling at us. We are trapped by our work schedules, the demands of family and friends, and the obligations in our home. As one tough day becomes another and another, we can be pulled into darkness and depression. We begin to wonder if life is really worth the price we are paying to live it. So like Harrison did almost five decades ago, at times we must step away, take a breath, and look around us. It is when we slow down that we can listen to the world's wonderful sounds rather than manmade noise, the kind words of friends and family, and the soft directives and assurance given by God.

George Harrison waited until he was at wit's end

to get away from his troubles; you should not let the pressures of life push you that far. You need to find a time each day when you do something you love. Even if it is only for five minutes, you need to play your favorite music, sing a song, read a few pages of a book, take a walk, or just sit out and enjoy the scenes going on around us. You can claim your piece of the sun in your home, on a park bench, at the beach, or walking the dog, but that small gift you give to yourself will help put everything else into perspective. Suddenly you will know what is important as well as what you can do without. You will also likely find that in that quiet time when you embrace a childlike spirit, you will hear God as well.

$\mathcal{T}$IE A YELLOW RIBBON

I received a tradition from the Lord, which I also handed on to you: on the night on which he was betrayed, the Lord Jesus took bread. After giving thanks, he broke it and said, "This is my body, which is for you; do this to remember me." He did the same thing with the cup, after they had eaten, saying, "This cup is the new covenant in my blood. Every time you drink it, do this to remember me." Every time you eat this bread and drink this cup, you broadcast the death of the Lord until he comes. —1 Corinthians 11:23-26

The Lord's Supper is one of those elements of faith that is often treated as ritual rather than a reminder. For many, it becomes such a routine that no thought is given to what the bread and cup represent. Yet perhaps no one tradition in Christian life is as sharp a reminder of what Jesus did for us or what that sacrifice should mean to us. Thus we need to focus on the act of communion as more than just another basic element of the church doctrine and instead make it personal.

There are conflicting stories on where the tradition of tying a yellow ribbon originated. Some historians trace it back as far as the Civil War. It is known that during the nineteenth century, some women wore a yellow ribbon in their hair to symbolize their love and support for someone serving in the US Cavalry. This was such a part of Western lore that a John Wayne movie was based on this tradition. Yet the story that likely inspired a hit song came from the 1960s and concerns a man who had been sentenced to prison. Upon his release, he caught a bus ride back to his hometown. He had instructed his wife to tie a yellow ribbon on an oak tree in their yard if she was willing to accept him back into her life. His eyes filled with tears when he saw the ribbon and knew he had been forgiven.

Irwin Levine and L. Russell Brown used that legend to fashion a song for Tony Orlando and Dawn. Its message of never forgetting was so universal that, in 1973, "Tie A Yellow Ribbon" reached #1 in the United States, Canada, New Zealand, Australia, and Great Britain.

No matter its origins, the yellow ribbon is a reminder of sacrifice and service. It is a symbol of love that survives the very worst that humanity has to throw at it. Like a light in a window, it is a visible statement that a person will not be forgotten and will always be welcomed home. To those who put out those yellow ribbons, that reminder constantly brings into sharp focus what the person missing from their home means to them.

As you next participate in the symbolic act of remembrance of the sacrifice of Christ, look at it not as just as a Christian ritual, but put yourself at the table with Jesus and his disciples. Look into the eyes of the man who was about to give his life for your sins and tell him that you will not forget what he did for you! Thus you have made it personal and made it real!

As Time Goes By

I know the plans I have in mind for you, declares the LORD; they are plans for peace, not disaster, to give you a future filled with hope. —Jeremiah 29:11

Outside of his hometown of Montclair, New Jersey, Herman Hupfeld is not a man much remembered today. In fact, even in 1920s and 1930s, when he penned several songs for New York musicals, Hupfeld was often dismissed as just another run of the mill tunesmith. Yet, beating the odds, one of his songs from the Broadway play *Everybody's Welcome*, while just a minor hit for Rudy Vallee in 1931, would find new life anchoring a legendary film and give Hupfeld an iconic number for the ages.

The story behind *Casablanca* is almost as interesting and compelling as the movie itself. When started in 1941, the film had no ending. A team of writers was still arguing about that element of the script, and with no finished script, Warner Brothers executives were wondering if the unique movie Hal Wallis was producing and Michael Curtiz was directing would ever get made. Yet somehow, in the midst of a myriad of problems, the writers came up with an ending, the movie was finished, and in the midst of the film, one of Herman Hupfeld's forgotten songs, "As Time Goes By," found a home.

In *Casablanca*, the character of Rick, played by Humphrey Bogart, was a cynic. His life was his own, and he saw no reason to do anything noble with it. For Rick, "As Time Goes By" symbolized the most wonderful moment of his life as well as his most tragic loss. When Rick heard "You must remember this," the memories become so profound that he went to pieces. And yet as time went by, Rick changed his cynical tune and was willing to sacrifice everything for the woman he loved and the country he left.

As a Christian, if someone were to ask you *What is the one thing you must remember about your faith?* what would you tell them? What brings God's love into focus?

When Paul was in prison, he wrote to his friends that he had never been happier. He was sure that God had a plan for his life and had put him into a place where he could best serve. Just like the modern proverb, Paul bloomed where he was planted. So, just like Paul, you must remember that Jesus died on the cross for you. You also need to remember the lessons He taught you through His stories and His life. And you should realize that God has promised He has a plan for your life if you will just follow His lead.

Just as Herman Hupfeld likely felt his contributions to music had been overlooked and those producing *Casablanca* wondered if the writers would finish the script, we are often lost as to God's plan for our lives. It is not always clear. But if we do our best at this moment, forget living selfishly, and start living for others, our contributions will be recognized, and our lives will have great value to not just ourselves but to others.

GIVE MY REGARDS TO BROADWAY

"Be careful that you don't practice your religion in front of people to draw their attention. If you do, you will have no reward from your Father who is in heaven. Whenever you give to the poor, don't blow your trumpet as the hypocrites do in the synagogues and in the streets so that they may get praise from people. I assure you, that's the only reward they'll get. But when you give to the poor, don't let your left hand know what your right hand is doing so that you may give to the poor in secret. Your Father who sees what you do in secret will reward you."
—Matthew 6:1-4

George M. Cohan was a musical legend. Few writers or performers brought so much energy and talent to the Broadway stage. Cohan wrote more than three hundred songs. Many of his hits were of such magnitude that they are still known a century after they were penned. The tunesmith also created more than fifty New York stage shows. From his birth to musical acting parents to his death in 1942, he lived to perform and constantly searched for a spotlight. Few men have ever had their name in lights more than this Rhode Island–born celebrity, and it is doubtful few relished it anymore than George M. Cohan.

His best-known composition is likely "Give My Regards to Broadway." It is almost as much biography as a formula stage tune. This number, written in 1904 for the musical *Little Johnny Jones*, has become the unofficial theme song for every musical star for the past century. And why not? For a theatrical performer, making a mark on the Broadway stage is more than a dream; it is a quest. To hear the crowds cheer and to see your name spelled out twenty feet high in lights is the ultimate thrill. It was a thrill Cohan knew and cherished for four decades. Yet, though their names weren't ever in lights, there were millions of "little people" necessary to assure George M. Cohan's rise to the top. And those folks are really the most valuable part of any successful Broadway show. They make up the stage crew, the theater staff, and the audience.

Jesus pointed out to both his followers and the religious authorities of His day that there was no place for scene stealing in the Lord's work. Anyone whose goal was to claim personal glory rather than put the spotlight on the kingdom was not living a true faith.

And perhaps that is why the success of the church is due not to superstars of the gospel but to the few who we most rarely notice—the Sunday school teachers, those who visit hospitals, those who quietly tithe, sing in the choir, greet visitors, or seek out the least of these in their communities and help them for no reason other than love.

Look around you today. Consider the best examples of living for Christ. Are their names spelled out in lights on church buildings? Are they demanding a spotlight during the services? Are they bragging about what they do for the Lord? Are they more concerned about taking the credit for doing God's work rather than putting the spotlight on Christ? Or are they just going about living out Matthew 25:35-40? Those who made your humble list are the real heroes of faith, and while there might not be any earthly fame or glory in joining them, there is plenty of room in their ranks for you.

His Eye Is On the Sparrow

Aren't two sparrows sold for a small coin? But not one of them will fall to the ground without your Father knowing about it already. Even the hairs of your head are all counted. Don't be afraid. You are worth more than many sparrows. —Matthew 10:29-31

In 1904, Civilla Martin, noted speaker and songwriter, was on a lecture tour that landed her in Elmira, New York. After addressing a local church congregation, she was asked to visit a homebound couple who had once been the congregation's anchors. Though she reluctantly accepted the invitation, it was a trip the composer of "God Will Take Care of You" dreaded. She was sure the sickly couple's home would be dark and foreboding and the age and illness that were attacking their bodies would have the same effect on their spirits. Yet, most of all, she dreaded giving up a few of her precious moments for something that was not on her schedule.

As Martin arrived at the home, she found the couple even more frail and ill than she expected, but they were anything but low in spirit. In fact, they were happier and more carefree than anyone Martin had seen in months. When she asked their secret, the woman lifted a shaky hand, pointed out the room's large open window, and merrily explained, "It's the birds, if God is watching them, then He is watching me too." Martin had been sitting within them for an hour and never noticed the sparrows. How many other things had she missed by focusing only on what she thought she had to do each day?

Many of us have our lives planned out down to the smallest detail. Our goals are so important that they keep us from even stopping to count our blessings. And when we fail to see our blessings is when doubts start to creep into our lives.

When Civilla Martin grudgingly gave up an hour of her life, she felt she was being punished. She was tired, and she had a number of other things on her to-do list that seemed far more important. Yet her detour inspired a song, "His Eye Is On the Sparrow," that has been treasured for a century, and it also gave the thirty-eight-year-old woman a new perspective on life. She no longer saw interruptions in her plans as punishment. In fact, she often opted to travel the road others avoided just to observe things others missed.

It is during the quiet times when life slows down that we usually see a power greater than our own at work. It is when we notice the smile on a child's face or the embrace of a couple in love that we begin to understand the gifts we have been given. It is when a detour takes us off our normal route that we usually experience something unforgettable. It is when we stop, look, and listen that we are inspired. Rather than dread the unexpected or unwelcomed deviations from your schedule, think of them as God giving you the opportunity to travel to a new place and see or hear something special He has been saving just for you.

$\mathcal{S}$ILENT NIGHT

She gave birth to her firstborn child, a son, wrapped him snugly, and laid him in a manger, because there was no place for them in the guestroom. —Luke 2:7

On December 24, 1818, a young, inexperienced priest at St. Nicholas Church in Oberndorf, Austria, faced a problem that threatened to spoil his first holiday worship service. The church's ancient organ would not play, and nothing he did could pull even a solitary note from the instrument. With the clock ticking and panic fueling his movements, he raced across town to share his story with his best friend. Franz Gruber calmed Father Joseph Mohr and then proposed they substitute a guitar for the broken organ. Mohr sadly shook his head explaining a guitar would not work with any of the Christmas music he'd picked out. The school teacher then suggested they write something new. As fortune would have it, Mohr remembered a poem he had penned two years before on a snowy walk through the woods. The two took that poem, set it to music, and saved the Christmas Eve service with their new song, "Silent Night."

The song was never intended to be used again; it was simply a stopgap measure to head off a disaster. And today we would likely not know "Silent Night" if a man had not come to fix the church organ. The traveling repairman inquired about music used on Christmas Eve, and Mohr played the new song for him. Over the next two decades, in the course of his work, the organ repairman took the composition to hundreds of churches all over Europe. Twenty years later, Joseph Mohr, who had almost forgotten about his song, was shocked when, walking by a large German church, he heard hundreds of voices singing "Silent Night."

"Silent Night" has become one of the world's best-known songs. It has been translated into more than a hundred languages and is a musical anchor of the holiday season. The inspired message found in its lyrics brings the first Christmas to life in ways that few other songs can. Yet the man who wrote it had nothing to do with the song being spread all over the world. Until he heard it while walking by that German church, he never realized the impact of his work. Joseph Mohr never served a huge congregation. He never became a bishop or a cardinal. He did not write books, tour the world, or speak in front of huge gatherings. On the surface, his life seemed to matter little. He was just a pastor trying his best to lead to his flock. But imagine the world without "Silent Night."

We do things that cause ripples in the ponds of life. Even if we don't know it, people are impacted by our actions and our words. Just like an organ repairman took "Silent Night" to the world, someone might be so influenced by what we do that they will share that story with hundreds of others. So we must be constantly aware of how we live our lives. In a world filled with negative influences, raging voices, and those preaching division, we need to be the person who reflects Christ in our words and deeds. The message of our lives might well become the song that touches millions we never meet.

$\mathscr{I}$ Walk the Line

"Go in through the narrow gate. The gate that leads to destruction is broad and the road wide, so many people enter through it. But the gate that leads to life is narrow and the road difficult, so few people find it." —Matthew 7:13-14

In 1956, Johnny Cash was a newlywed and performing in Gladewater, Texas. While killing time backstage, he picked up a piece of paper and pen and scratched out a pledge of faithfulness. The words were intended to provide assurance to his new bride that he could be trusted, but as he studied his heartfelt prose, it dawned on him this had song potential. Marrying his words to a chord progression he had written while serving in the military, Cash created what would become his signature song, "I Walk the Line."

Like many, Cash had problems walking the line. He succumbed to temptations several times during his career. And when he failed to walk the line, others followed. Over the years, members of his group often joined the "Man in Black" in his detours and thus were caught in a web of various addictions. After a great deal of tragedy and personal loss, Cash turned his life around. Many of his friends, sadly, did not.

There is nothing easier than falling to temptations. It can begin with a running leap, but most people stray using small steps. We try something that seems just a little bit wrong first, and then we move into something a bit more wrong. It is not much different than setting the cruise control of your car at three miles over the speed limit and justifying it because so many others are going faster. But as more and more cars pass your car, it becomes easier to move the cruise up another mile or two. Soon you are going far faster than you ever intended, and the margin for error is much smaller. Yet if you never have a speed-related accident or get caught by the police, then what difference does it make? Who is hurt?

In the 1960s, a seemingly sweet TV ad showed a little boy following his father around. When the father did something, the boy would imitate him. The commercial showed the pair painting the house, washing the family car, and throwing rocks. Then the father sat down under a tree, lit a cigarette, and tossed the pack on the ground. The commercial spot ended with the small child picking up the pack and reaching for a cigarette.

There are people looking to us to understand what is and what is not acceptable. They depend upon us to guide them in a way that will lead them safely through the trials of life. If we bend the rules just a tiny bit, then it might not keep us from reaching our ultimate destination, but those who are observing us might be thrown so far off course that they never find their way home. Thus, for the sake of the world, it is vital we Christians walk the line.

You Are So Beautiful to Me

Treat people in the same way that you want them to treat you.
—Luke 6:31

Dennis Wilson is best remembered as the Beach Boys' drummer and brother of founding Beach Boy members Carl and Brian. He was in his teens when the band took off and, therefore, lived almost all of his adult life in the spotlight. Thus he was naturally invited to all the key social events and was at a party with soul singer Billy Preston when, during the course of a conversation trying to define the parameters of beauty, he came up with an idea for a song. It took Wilson and Preston just a few minutes to pen an unforgettable ballad that in simple but haunting prose spoke of a love that framed everything in beauty.

"You Are So Beautiful to Me" has been cut by scores of artists in every genre from soul to pop. Until his death, Wilson employed the number as a way of thanking the Beach Boys' audiences for being so good to the group.

When I was in high school, there was a girl with developmental disabilities who was often picked on by the supposed cool kids in my class. Though she might have not understood the reason for their actions, she felt the pain as the best-looking boys and even some of the most popular girls teased her. I could see the hope written on her face as she thought she was being accepted and then the hurt in her eyes when she figured out she was being pranked again. This girl was from a poor family, she had limited abilities, and she was very plain. But, if the bullies had taken a few minutes to actually speak to her, they would have found a loving spirit hidden beneath her tangled hair and ragged clothes. As I now look back on this trusting girl, I realize she was really beautiful in ways only the wise can see. She never gave up on being accepted and always forgave those who hurt her. That description sounds a lot like someone who walked the earth 2,000 years ago.

"You Are So Beautiful to Me" is about realized potential. The lyrics speak of a love that transformed a plain woman into a beauty of such magnitude as to defy description. Love has the power to do that and more. It can take a person who believes he or she has little value and make him or her the most confident person on earth. But to get love, you have to give love. If all you give is ugliness to others, then you will be ugly too.

I can now look back at those I went to school with and see them in a new light. Those who learned to accept and respect others, those who learned to embrace people rather than abuse them, grew to become some the most beautiful souls in the world. Their beauty is a product of what is in their hearts. It is the kind that needs no cosmetic surgery. In fact, they actually grow more beautiful with age. Rather than make fun of or torment the "least of these," like my classmate, they embrace them. Why? They reflect Christ, and that is what Jesus would do. To find out how beautiful you are, don't bother looking in the mirror. Instead look into the eyes of those who know you. What you see there defines who you really are!

$\mathscr{M}$IDNIGHT TRAIN TO GEORGIA

"I will get up and go to my father, and say to him, 'Father, I have sinned against heaven and against you. I no longer deserve to be called your son. Take me on as one of your hired hands.' So he got up and went to his father. While he was still a long way off, his father saw him and was moved with compassion. His father ran to him, hugged him, and kissed him. Then his son said, 'Father, I have sinned against heaven and against you. I no longer deserve to be called your son.'" —Luke 15:18-21

Most people who listen to Gladys Knight and the Pips most famous hit, "Midnight Train to Georgia" sing the back-up vocals rather than the lead. There is just something about the line "Superstar but he didn't get far" that is irresistible. Yet, as one intently listens to this golden oldie's lyrics, something else jumps out. In just a bit over three minutes, this song tells the story of a man with big dreams who finds he doesn't have what he needs to cut it in Los Angeles and is therefore forced to take his tattered reputation back to the small town where he was raised. Written by Jim Weatherly, who had already penned a number of country music hits, this soul single won a Grammy and topped the charts in 1973.

"Midnight Train to Georgia" is a modern take on one of the most famous of Christ's parables. Yet in this case, the humbled wanderer doesn't come back alone. A woman whose love is not tied to his success or acclaim accompanies him. She stands by and accepts this supposed failure simply because of what he is. In other words, she knows his heart.

After squandering his inheritance, the Bible's prodigal son's life has so completely collapsed that he loses everything he owns and is forced to take the lowest form of work in the world. Completely humbled, he makes the longest trip of his life alone. His destination is one that leads to his falling on the ground and admitting he has been a fool.

Our reaction to the prodigals in our life is one of the key barometers of the depth of our faith. If we are like Christ, then we immediately forgive them. We don't ask them to humble themselves or beg for our acceptance. In fact we don't extract a toll, but instead we celebrate their return by making sure they know how much they mean to us and that our love outweighs all the wrongs they have done.

Forgiveness and acceptance go hand in hand and are so important that the Bible is filled with stories of people, from David to Saul, who had miserably failed only to be embraced and unconditionally loved by God. Is there someone in your life who would come home if they knew you would open your arms to their return? Maybe it is time for you to be like woman in "Midnight Train to Georgia" and the father in the story of the prodigal son and make their humbling homecoming trip a bit easier by walking some of the steps with them.

$\mathscr{S}$INGING IN THE RAIN

Just as the rain and the snow come down from the sky and don't return there without watering the earth, making it conceive and yield plants and providing seed to the sower and food to the eater, so is my word that comes from my mouth; it does not return to me empty. Instead, it does what I want, and accomplishes what I intend. —Isaiah 55:10-11

Arthur Freed penned the optimistic lyrics for "Singing in the Rain" during the Roaring Twenties. Published in 1929, it jumped onto the hit parade and was employed in one of the first movie musicals. Even when the world plunged into the Great Depression, the optimistic song continued to be used in a number of films throughout the next decade, including Judy Garland's *Little Nellie Kelly* in 1940. Yet it was in a 1952 Technicolor classic where the song really made its mark.

Singing in the Rain is one of the most popular motion pictures of all time. The scene in which Gene Kelly dances in a downpour while singing the title song has become an iconic number that defines the musical movie genre. Kelly's exuberance revealed in that number embraces a man's joy in ways that seem to lift the spirits of all who view the movie.

There is a saying that goes, "Attitude is everything." Though He might have not said it the same way, Jesus shared similar sentiments with men and women during his days on earth. Christ celebrated good attitudes while condemning those committed to judging others. While it is easy to picture children dancing around Christ, it would be hard to imagine one of the Pharisees racing through the streets joyfully singing a song of happiness. The attitude of the Pharisees would have prevented this kind of reaction. And that was one of the roadblocks that kept them from seeing what Jesus was offering. Many were far too busy complaining to celebrate the blessing they had been given.

Christ brought not just peace and understanding but joy to the world. Imagine the reaction of the lepers He cured. Consider the response of the lame who were healed or the dead who were raised. If we embrace the attitude of a Pharisee, then we will always wish for something else and always feel like what is before us is simply not enough. We will not only never see the beauty and smell the freshness of a rainy day but also see too much fault around us to ever find a reason to dance or sing. Consider the old children's song, "(I've Got the Joy, Joy, Joy, Joy) Down in My Heart." That song embraces everything we have to celebrate about our faith. We are saved, death has been beaten, the grave cannot hold our spirits, and the burdens of our lives can be shared with the maker of the universe. If that doesn't bring the kind of joy that Gene Kelly displayed in the film *Singing in the Rain*, then what does? So no matter the problems that face you now, no matter the storms that roll through your life, you still have something to sing about. After all, even when it is raining, you have a future that stretches on without end, and you will spend it with the God who loves you more than you can fathom.

We've Only Just Begun

In the beginning was the Word and the Word was with God and the Word was God. —John 1:1

When he wrote the lyrics to "We've Only Just Begun," Paul Williams was not looking at godly love but at the love of a couple for each other. The song's message didn't outline the problems each newly married couple faces but embraced the optimism of building something meaningful together. No longer were the events of the past important, but thanks to love, a joyous future awaited.

When Williams created the lyrics, he fully understood the blessings of opportunity. A small man who was limited in many areas by his short stature, he found a place where size didn't matter and became a giant. With each new day, his ideas poured into music-touched hearts, and he was able to overcome the shortsightedness of a world that often viewed promise based purely on appearance or athletic talent. Maybe that is the reason Williams wrote so often about the potential for everyone to find lasting acceptance and love.

Though they were not the first to record it, the Carpenters, with Richard's arrangement and Karen's vocal, took the song to the top of the charts. Within weeks of its release, "We've Only Just Begun" was embraced my thousands of couples as the story of their love and marriage.

John could have started his Gospel with the phrase, "We have only just begun", and in a way, he did. As he began to tell the story of Jesus's life, he didn't focus on a birth in a manger but harkened back to the first verse in the Bible. Many feel cheated because John didn't give us new details on the first Christmas, but another look proves that his beginning was perfect. Jesus came to offer us a second chance. He gave us a life beyond the law based not on rigid rules but on free flowing grace. With each sunrise, we have a chance to be a new creation where all the baggage we have carried with us is lifted, and we start with a clean slate. No matter our age or station in life, we can begin again.

Today is a great day for a fresh start. It is a wonderful time to commit to making changes that will help us walk in Christ's footsteps. By simply beginning again, we are committing to being like Jesus, the love and acceptance we felt when He came into our hearts can grow and give us more understanding of our calling in life.

With a list of hits that includes "Just an Old Fashioned Love Song," "The Rainbow Connection," "Evergreen," and "We've Only Just Begun," Paul Williams provided a model of what an optimistic point of view coupled to accepting a calling can accomplish. But to find both of those essential elements needed for happiness, we have to cast off what is holding us back and forget the world's small view of our potential. When we do that and accept God's chance to start all over again, we can accomplish more than we can imagine.

$\mathscr{I}$F I HAD A HAMMER

Whatever you do, do it from the heart for the Lord and not for people. You know that you will receive an inheritance as a reward. You serve the Lord Christ. —Colossians 3:23-24

"If I Had a Hammer," written by folk singer Pete Seegar and Lee Hays, was first recorded by The Weavers in 1949. Yet the timing for a number like this was completely wrong. Therefore the song, with its symbolic lyrics alluding to bringing equality and justice to everyone no matter race or station in life, would not become a hit until the 1960s when recorded by Peter, Paul, and Mary. Though almost childlike in presentation, this version of "If I Had a Hammer" would become a musical anthem for the Civil Rights movement.

Throughout its simple and repetitious verses, the song embraces a theme of constructing an ideal world by using various tools. These seemingly fundamental elements of everyday life were to alert people of danger while pushing brotherly love as the cure for a corrupt world's ills. The hammer represented justice, the bell represented freedom, and the love stood for acceptance.

It wouldn't take much rewriting to make "If I Had a Hammer" a Christian hymn. After all, we are to build God's kingdom here on earth, and that requires justice, freedom, and love. But what other tools could be used to create this new kingdom?

We might want to begin with faith. Jesus assured us that even childlike faith could move mountains. We were also warned that without faith works were dead. So our first verse needs to embrace faith as the cornerstone of our Christian endeavors.

Next we must turn to prayer. Jesus emphasized the importance of prayer and even gave us a model to use when speaking to God. Prayer is a way that we can reach the Lord and He can reach us. So for faith to truly grow, we must make prayer a habit that is as much a routine as breathing.

Every good builder works from a plan. The plans for building a bit of heaven on earth can be found in the Bible. So studying the Scripture is essential for us to find the knowledge and wisdom we need when confronting problems.

And the final element needed to compose a new version of "If I Had a Hammer" mirrors what Seegar and Hays wrote so many years ago—love. It is almost impossible to reach out to "the least of these" if we don't feel God's love in our hearts. As Paul pointed out, the strongest and most powerful of all our emotions is love. So we have to love those around us to fully engage ourselves in helping them. Today is a good day to put our faith into action by praying, studying, and loving. If we live by that simple theme, we will lift others' burdens, bring fulfillment to our own lives, make the world a bit better, and really have something to sing about.

$\mathscr{B}$ICYCLE BUILT
FOR TWO

Two are better than one because they have a good return for their hard work. —Ecclesiastes 4:9

In 1892, Harry Dacre was shocked upon immigrating to the United States to find that custom officials demanded he pay import duties on the bicycle he'd brought with him from England. As close friend William Jerome watched the incredulous Dacre pay the fee, he quipped, "It's lucky you didn't bring a bicycle built for two or you would have to pay double duty." That joke took root as a song idea, and Dacre penned "Daisy Bell," which is now known as "Bicycle Built For Two." With the fad of bicycling sweeping the world, Dacre's song about love and teamwork became a worldwide hit almost before the immigrant could unpack his bags.

"Bicycle Built for Two" symbolizes marriage in a way few songs ever have. Its lyrics proclaimed money or status had nothing to do with experiencing true happiness. The song also hinted that for love to prosper the two parties had to work together. This is not just true in love; it is true for every facet of life.

One of the first things Christ did in his ministry was form a team. The twelve who joined this group had little in common. They came from different professions and backgrounds and had ranging interests. As we read in the Bible, it was not always easy to keep these dozen folks focused on the same goal or even going in a common direction. But when they drew together, they performed something miraculous. They shared the story of Christ in such a way it swept out of the Middle East and was taken to every corner of the globe. Today we know their names not because of what they did alone but because they chose to be part of a team.

What teams are you on right now? For most the first team they are a part of is a family. For many the next team might be school. The education experience often gives us a chance to be on a wide variety of other teams from sports to music to drama to academics. As we grow, our teams might include church, work, and civic clubs. Each of our experiences with these teams teaches us a great deal about how teamwork plays a large part in success. We discover that if the team members are not pulling together, then the team usually fails, and those who on that team are often left disillusioned, frustrated, and unhappy.

"Bicycle Built for Two" is a simple song propelled by an elementary concept—two working together with the same goal can more easily reach that goal. The key is working together. What teams are you a part of? What part do you play on those teams? Are you giving your all? Are you pulling your weight? What more can you do to help your team, be it family, friends, coworkers, or church members, reach their goals? If you give your all for your teams, then you will find the members of those teams will be there to give their all for you when you need them most. And that is what makes being a part of a team vital in both the Christian world and secular life. We have those to help us through the tough days and celebrate with us the good times too.

In the Good Old Summertime

He said to them, "Go into the whole world and proclaim the good news to every creature." —Mark 16:15

More than one hundred ten years ago, George Evans and Ren Shields were enjoying the many wonders of a New York City summer. It was a time when America was awash with optimism as immigrants from all over the world flocked to the United States bringing their varied interests and culture with them. The city was also quickly becoming the world's cultural mecca. The songs the world was singing were now coming from Tin Pan Alley rather than Berlin, Vienna, Paris, or London. America had grown up and was on the verge of greatness.

As the songwriters excitedly spoke of their hopes for this new age, they also thought about what was been lost. Cars were replacing wagons, society was much more mobile, movies were predicted to take

the place of plays, and sitting on the porch and talking seemed as old fashioned as a European waltz.
Their contrasting the way things were to the way
they used to be led to the creation of "In the Good
Old Summertime." Evans and Shields's composition
would set sheet music sales records and become one
of the first huge hits of recorded music.

Even today, many look back nostalgically on the
way things used to be. They seem to long for the
days before television and Internet, back to a time
when everyone wrote letters, most folks sat under
trees and talked with their neighbors, a long trip was
a few hundred miles, and most died just a few miles
from where they were born. But if that was the good
old summertime, what does that make today? Are
things now so bad and hopeless we are suffering
through history's cold, ugly winter?

Life is all about perspective and change. And it is
how we deal with change that determines perspective.
Were the good old days that wonderful without air
conditioning, ease of travel, and the medical marvels
we have today? Aren't you glad you live in a country
that is not divided racially and that the door to opportunity is open for millions who were denied their
rights in the past? And that is just the beginning. In
truth, for Christians now is the good old summertime!

In the past, we might have been able to share our faith only within our city limits, but today there are no limits. Thanks to the modern age of travel, cheap cell phone plans, and the Internet, we live in an age where it is never been easier to take the gospel to the whole world. Only our perspective or attitude can hold us back from reaching people in every corner of the planet. I imagine Paul would have been so excited to have this opportunity, and so should we. So rather than look back longingly, we need to embrace the opportunity of this moment. We must open the channels technology has given us, embrace the blessings of a modern age, and find new ways to share our faith.

CELEBRATION

Let them praise God's name with dance; let them sing God's praise with the drum and lyre! —Psalm 149:3

Celebrating with music has been a universal facet of human life since the beginning. It seems that songs are often the best way for most to fully voice our joy. Music allows individuals to become emotional without embarrassment as it provides a vehicle for movement and expression. It is such a vital facet of life that it can be argued no special occasion is complete without it.

Imagine for a moment a world without music. Consider what it would be like to have no songs in church or carols at Christmas. Imagine movies without background themes or radio that was all talk. Consider a birthday with candles but no chorus of "Happy Birthday to You." In a world without music, we would have never heard the voices of Frank, Bing, or Elvis or known the compositions of Mozart or Bach. There would be no halftime shows at football games, no concerts, and no dances. There would be no national anthems or lullabies. A world without music is a much different, much more sobering, and a far sadder place.

A thousand years ago during the advent season, clerics asked their parishioners to consider what life would be like if Jesus had never come to earth. The faithful were to think about what Christ meant to them personally. As they thought about their faith, it offered them a chance to refocus on how Jesus had really changed their lives. What would life be without the story of Christ, the parables, the Lord's Prayer, and the assurance of heaven?

In 1980, disco music was at the end of its short reign on radio. Yet as the genre died, it produced one final monster hit that still resonates in the public consciousness. Written as a group project by the American pop/jazz band Kool & the Gang, the upbeat lyrics of "Celebration" combined with an infectious melody still gets people on their feet whenever it is played.

About the time Kool & the Gang were getting folks up to sing and dance to "Celebration," gospel legends Bill and Gloria Gaither composed an inspirational song that reframed Christ's life in a new way. In the Gaithers' "God Gave the Song," the couple proposed the real reason for celebration didn't arrive until Jesus was born. The lyrics went further to proclaim the fact that when Christ rose from the grave, this God-given song became even more powerful.

If you know Christ as Lord, then there is a reason to celebrate. If He is in your heart and guiding your life, then others have cause to sing because they also feel His touch in your touch. Music and Jesus—a combination that should always put us in the mood to smile and sing and become a part of the celebration of life, hope, joy, and faith!

WHAT A WONDERFUL WORLD

We live by faith and not by sight. —2 Corinthians 5:7

The late sixties was not an optimistic period in American history. It seemed to many that the entire fabric of culture was being ripped asunder. The Vietnam War had become so unpopular that a younger generation was viewing the military and government leaders as their enemies. The Civil Rights movement was creating and exposing deep wounds as well. Many were questioning if it was even wise to bring a child into the world during these troubling times.

While others were penning songs echoing a younger generation's resentment and rebellion, veteran tunesmiths Bob Thiele and George David Weiss took a much different route. They saw the pain and suffering and felt the mistrust and fear, but they also looked beyond those images and observed something much deeper afoot. They saw a new generation that deeply valued life and equality and perceived a future filled with wonder and hope where races would find common ground and truth would no longer be reserved just for those who made the rules. With that in mind, the writers penned "What a Wonderful World."

This new song was not one that many artists were initially drawn to. With no contemporary music stars lining up to cut it, Thiele and Weiss offered it to Tony Bennett. When Bennett turned it down, it was given to Louis Armstrong. Because had grown up during segregation, the black jazz trumpeter fully believed the best was yet to come. Yet Armstrong's record sold just 1,000 copies in the United States during its initial release. It was only when "What a Wonderful World" was revived on the British charts that the sixty-eight-year-old Armstrong saw his native country embrace his hopeful recording.

Christians often see the church in the same light millions saw the world in the late sixties. Many feel the best days for faith are in the past. They look at new babies in a congregation and pity them because they were not alive during the "Golden Days of Worship." Yet, if we look back in history, we find that a hundred years ago millions of Christians had the same viewpoint feeling faith's best days were led by

Billy Sunday and Dwight Moody. In the 1500s, Martin Luther shook things up to such an extent many bemoaned the death of faith then too. Go back twenty centuries and Jewish religious leaders felt things were a lot better before Christ offered a new perspective.

We reflect what we feel. If we act as though the world is going to hell in a handbasket, then we show that on our face and with our words. If we choose to see the potential in the moment, then we are enthusiastic about what the new generation will experience in their lives. Those in the first generation of the church were optimistic about the future. Paul, Timothy, and others believed, in spite of the hardships and persecution, better days were coming. With that mind-set, they built Christianity. With the freedoms we have today, certainly we can find reasons for hope now and in the future as well.

$\mathscr{U}$NFORGETTABLE

Pray like this: Our Father who is in heaven, uphold the holiness of your name. Bring in your kingdom so that your will is done on earth as it's done in heaven. Give us the bread we need for today. Forgive us for the ways we have wronged you, just as we also forgive those who have wronged us. And don't lead us into temptation, but rescue us from the evil one. —Matthew 6:9-13

Jesus gave us a pattern for speaking to God that most of us have memorized. We can easily recite each of the words in the King James version of the Lord's Prayer. Thus, for hundreds of millions, it is unforgettable. But knowing the words and actually feeling them are two different things. Is the prayer just a bunch of phrases said without emotion or meaning or does the message resonate in our hearts and inspire our actions?

In 1951, Irving Gordon wrote a song about love he called "Uncomparable." While the publisher felt Gordon's song had promise, they were not excited by his grammatically incorrect title. Back at his desk, Gordon scratched through uncomparable and penciled in unforgettable. Nat King Cole, one of the first African-American singers to gain acceptance on radio and find an audience that crossed racial lines, cut "Unforgettable," and his smooth style made the record a huge hit.

Most of us know the story of Christ's life, death, and resurrection as well as we know the details of our own experience. We can talk about Jesus the boy in the temple astounding the priests. We know about the healed lepers, the woman at the well, and Zacchaeus in the tree. We certainly know about the birth in the manger and death on the cross. But are they like that memorized prayer that no longer carries emotion or weight?

The composer of "Were You There When They Crucified My Lord" was an American slave. Perhaps his lack of freedom allowed him to better understand and fully appreciate Jesus' suffering on the cross. After all, the Savior loved the slave as much as the master. Thus, when the writer sang the words, he was there witnessing Jesus on the cross, seeing the blood, and feeling the pain as well as experiencing the shame. He was also there when Christ rose from the grave. This thought brought the slave so much

hope that his eyes likely filled with tears and voice probably choked with emotion.

Is your faith emotional? Does it move in three dimensions, or is it just a bunch of words and stories that lay flat on the page? To be unforgettable, it has to resonate in your mind and your soul. For most, it only becomes that meaningful and real when they do more than learn the stories—they live them. Putting your faith to work allows Christ to become more real. It is only when you become His hands on earth that He will become unforgettable and truly change your life. Christianity needs you to not just know the words but to walk the walk today.

$\mathscr{Y}$OU'LL NEVER WALK ALONE

The LORD is my shepherd. I lack nothing. He lets me rest in grassy meadows; he leads me to restful waters; he keeps me alive. He guides me in proper paths for the sake of his good name. Even when I walk through the darkest valley, I fear no danger because you are with me. Your rod and your staff—they protect me. You set a table for me right in front of my enemies. You bathe my head in oil; my cup is so full it spills over! Yes, goodness and faithful love will pursue me all the days of my life, and I will live in the LORD's house as long as I live. —Psalm 23:1-6

In 1945, Americans understood a great deal about teamwork. The nation had come together to fight a war on two fronts with millions serving in combat overseas and people of all ages working to supply the soldiers, sailors, and marines with everything from planes and k-rations to uniforms. On top of that, almost every household in the nation was sacrificing by conserving and recycling. It was a time when team was not just understood; it was the acknowledged way to accomplish great things.

It is not known if Rogers and Hammerstein were considering the teamwork shown during the war when they created the musical *Carousel*, but what can't be doubted is whether the songwriters fully understood that working together made them much stronger than trying to go it alone. They knew from experience that no Broadway production could be successful without a team of everything from actors to stagehands combining talents for a common goal.

The hit song from *Carousel* was "You'll Never Walk Alone." The number was meant to show that even widows or orphans could still feel the presence and support of those who had died. The song not only presented an inspirational standard for the leads to perform but also emphasized the musical's concept of redemption.

The words of the most famous verses found in the book of Psalms echo the lyrics of the popular Broadway show tune. No matter what challenges we face and no matter how alone we feel, God is with us each step of the way. Therefore we are never really walking alone through any period of our life. But for those without faith, times of trial can seem overwhelming. What can we do for those who don't know the Lord is with them? How can we help those who simply can't feel His presence?

In your world, there are those who have been abused, neglected, and unloved. They carry deep scars and cling to shallow self-confidence. They often feel they don't deserve to ask anyone to help them with their problems or share their load. You likely won't be able to reach them with a simple word-based testimony. They won't be ready to accept that God supports and loves them. They might not be ready to admit the Lord is real. If this is the case, then they must see Christ in you. And that means you need to step into their world and find a way to walk with them through their valleys and carry them up their mountains. Then they might learn what motivated your actions and come to feel and know the One who makes sure you never walk alone.

$\mathcal{L}$OVE ME TENDER

Love the LORD your God with all your heart, all your being, and all your strength. —Deuteronomy 6:5

Christians who love do so gently and without judgment. They are like Christ in that they don't set conditions for love. They never believe that another person is unworthy of love. Christians believe that even if they go into a situation unsure of their ability to love, they should allow Jesus to shine through their actions. If they do so, they will come to find love in places they hadn't expected it and be able to show and give love in ways they couldn't fathom.

C. S. Lewis once wrote, "Do not waste time bothering whether you love your neighbor; act as if you did. As soon as we do this we find one of the great secrets. When you are behaving as if you loved someone you will presently come to love him."

In 1956, Hollywood decided to see if movie audiences would love Elvis Presley as much as music fans did. In his initial film role, the singer was cast in a

Western called *The Reno Brothers*. The producers decided they needed a quartet of songs to please Presley's fans and called in one of industry's most experienced writers, Ken Darby, to pen them. Darby, who had spent years working with the top stars in entertainment and was coming off doing the arrangements for *The King and I*, felt he was taking a step down when asked to share his talents with a rock and roller. Thus, to disguise his role in the film, he assigned his wife's name to the musical score. As the movie's title was changed to one of the songs he composed, and "Love Me Tender" sold millions of records, he might have later regretted not putting his name on the film's score. Yet his act of giving another credit for his work reflected how most define true love. After all, in the Bible it clearly points out that love is about giving much more than taking.

Loving us tenderly is what Jesus did and what He expects us to do today. When we show Christian love, we need to also defer credit to the One who first showed us love. When we modestly point to Jesus as the author of the love that flows through us, we chart a course for others to see the joy and feel the power of accepting Christ as Savior. We also put them in a position to get what they most need in life—love!

No one loved more unconditionally than Mother

Teresa. After ministering to India's "untouchables" she said, "The hunger for love is much more difficult to remove than the hunger for bread." Just like the poorest of the poor in India, everyone needs love even more deeply than they need food. Christ gave love freely to the woman at the well, lepers, and tax collectors. He asked nothing back in return. That is the kind of tender and unconditional love we must show as well. After all, love is the one gift we can give away that never runs out. The more love we give the more it is returned. Therefore it is the best investment we will ever make on this earth.

⁊HIS LITTLE LIGHT
OF MINE

Neither do people light a lamp and put it under a basket.
Instead, they put it on top of a lampstand, and it shines on all
who are in the house. In the same way, let your light shine
before people, so they can see the good things you do and praise
your Father who is in heaven. —Matthew 5:15-16

There are many Christians who light a candle each time they pray for someone. To those who light that candle, the tiny flame represents the power of hope and prayer. It also reminds the one praying that Jesus was the light of the world and that by sharing our faith in Him we are bringing light into the darkest places on the planet.

Though he died more than twenty years before "This Little Light of Mine" was written, the nineteenth century's greatest evangelist, Dwight L. Moody, deserves at least a part of the credit for the creation of this famous children's song. It was Moody who led the great American revival movement and created the Moody Bible Institute that opened doors to both those seeking to preach as well as those yearning to compose. It was in that center of learning that Harry Dixon Loes found the light needed to deepen his knowledge of faith and music.

During his studies, Loes was struck by the significance of three different references to light in the New Testament. As he began to compose a new song, he no doubt also considered the light he had seen spread through those associated with Moody. Using light as an inspiration and coupling it to a melody that carried the feel of a spiritual, Loes wrote "This Little Light of Mine". Yet the song, which is today almost universally known, took a while to take off. Although written in 1920, it would be in the days just before World War II that churches began to adopt "This Little Light of Mine" as a part of Sunday school programs. Within a decade, Loes's song was translated into scores of languages and sung all over the globe.

The way "This Little Light of Mine" spread from one person to another from one community to another from one country to another reflects the power of the light we carry in our hearts. But for that light to make an impact, it must be shared. Martin Luther tied a candle on his Christmas tree and explained to his children that the world was a dark and unforgiving place until Jesus came into the world. He then pointed to the candle on the tree as representing the light that came into the world with Christ. That was the beginning of Christmas lights. In a similar way "This Little Light of Mine" asks the singer to share faith and inspiration with the world and do that by proudly showing the light of Christ in his or her life.

We reach others one life at time. We share with them the light, and it ignites their passion to share it with others. We can do it through a song, a prayer, a good deed, or with a word, but we can't do it unless we are willing to allow our faith to be seen. We must shine!

$\mathscr{E}$VERYTHING IS BEAUTIFUL

Whatever you do, do it from the heart for the Lord and not for people. —*Colossians 3:23*

In 1970, Ray Stevens was known as one of the clown princes of entertainment. His hit singles were funny, off-the-wall compositions that bordered on bizarre. He largely took elements of pop culture and poked fun at whatever was the current hot fad. Therefore it was somewhat shocking when Stevens wrote and released a song that seemed to dramatically deviate from what had made him famous. Yet, when taken against the backdrop of time, perhaps "Everything Is Beautiful" was more than just a dynamic ballad trumpeting a new way of looking at beauty; it might have also been a mirror whose lyrics caused society to study a not-so-pretty reflection of prejudice and exclusion.

As Stevens penned "Everything Is Beautiful," America was dealing with the civil rights movement and the integration of African Americans into the country's culture. Ugly words were being hurled, and vile acts were a part of this period in history. Stevens, a deep, sensitive man, was moved by the images of those hurt by these actions. Thus he was in the perfect frame of mind to write a song showing the way people should see the world.

"Everything Is Beautiful" is a colorless song filled with color and a simple number peppered with great depth. Essentially Stevens celebrated the differences of humans while pointing out that in God's eyes each race is seen in the same way. He further explained that God made each person unique; therefore, they are beautiful in ways that those who love the Lord should more easily be able to see. Stevens essentially put the fault of not seeing the beauty in others squarely on the shoulders of those who were not allowing God to direct their thoughts and actions. So not only was their vision flawed but also their hearts.

Jesus didn't view people as those around him did. While others saw the ugliness of sin, he saw the beauty of life that could be transformed. When others ran from those with horrible diseases, he ran to them to offer compassion. Where others pushed away those of a different race of faith, he opened his arms to them.

Do you judge people based on human standards? Do you write those off who are too thin or too fat or too tall or too thin? Do you look at a person who is living in what you consider great sin and turn your back on them? Do you look beyond the color of skin or physical attractiveness and see the beauty that God placed in that person?

In his hit song, Ray Stevens asked his audience to evaluate how they judged others. He demanded they take a second look at those they had written off. In other words, he begged them to see people as Jesus did. Those who embraced the message in Stevens' Grammy-winning "Everything Is Beautiful" opened their eyes and hearts to a much more beautiful world. This is a world that is open to all who have the vision of Christ.

ℐESUS LOVES THE LITTLE CHILDREN

Some people brought children to Jesus so that he would place his hands on them and pray. But the disciples scolded them. "Allow the children to come to me," Jesus said. "Don't forbid them, because the kingdom of heaven belongs to people like these children." Then he blessed the children and went away from there. —Matthew 19:13-15

"Jesus Loves the Little Children" was no doubt inspired by those verses in Matthew or perhaps the art created around the image of Jesus surrounded by children. Though the writer of Matthew didn't go into great detail on this episode in Christ's life, there is a comforting theme that emerges from his short description of the event. It seems that Jesus was not only responsive to children but also fascinated by them. That speaks volumes about the way Christians need to live today.

During Jesus' time on earth, children were often pushed to the side. They were not privy to the conversations and dealings of adults. They were expected not to bother elders, especially those as important as Christ. Yet once again, Jesus turned the tables on the conventions of the era when he took time from his busy schedule to visit with these kids. Imagine the reaction of the religious leaders. They would have never considered such an act. Even Jesus' own disciples were shocked by Christ's behavior and likely surprised by His explanation. How was that possible? These were children; they saw things simply and without the filter provided by society and history! And that was the lesson most missed then and still miss today.

C. Herbert Woolston is a somewhat mysterious figure. Little is known about the Chicago native. He was born in the years leading up to the Civil War and died not long before the Great Depression. His name would have likely been lost forever if he hadn't reworked the lyrics of an obscure children's prayer and coupled them to the music of a George Root tune called "Tramp, Tramp, Tramp." This unique marriage of prayerful lyrics and a war march tune created the hauntingly beautiful "Jesus Loves the Little Children."

For his day, Woolston must have been a forward-thinking man. His lyrics crossed racial lines at a time when ethnic groups were divided by both culture and law. The writer presented a Jesus willing to bring races together in a way that didn't favor one over the other. That kind of thinking would have been shocking a hundred years ago. So when released, "Jesus Loves the Little Children" likely made the establishment of its day just as uncomfortable as did Jesus when he opened his arms to children

It is easy to sing the lyrics to "Jesus Loves the Little Children," but it is much harder to actually practice them. We live in a world where prejudice is still real. Thus Christians must strive to be as colorblind as was Christ. When that kind of thinking is incorporated into the way we live, something else happens. Children flocked to Christ. They did so because they knew He would not unfairly judge them on the standards of that time. Once we adopt the higher standards of love set by Jesus, people will sense our hearts and flock to us as well.

ℋappy Trails to You

"Therefore, go and make disciples of all nations, baptizing them in the name of the Father and of the Son and of the Holy Spirit, teaching them to obey everything that I've commanded you. Look, I myself will be with you every day until the end of this present age." —Matthew 28:19-20

In his letters to the early churches, Paul often wrote about how much the prayers, kind words, and spiritual support meant to him. These early Christians provided the apostle with the lift he needed to continue his often dangerous work of spreading the gospel. Even for us today, it is much easier to face life's trials when the good wishes of friends follow us each step of the way.

Dale Evans was the Queen of the West to a generation of baby boomers. Married to cowboy movie star Roy Rogers, Evans was more than an actress; she was a deeply spiritual woman who shared her faith with her friends and fans. She was also an author and songwriter. It was the latter where she might well have had the greatest lasting impact. Though she wrote several hits, it would be one she penned for the couple's television and radio programs that has most stood the test of time.

A song written by western singer Foy Willing inspired "Happy Trails." Evans borrowed Willing's title and first few notes and created a musical farewell that became a bestseller. "Happy Trails" was an optimistic anthem of hope that subtly taught a spiritual lesson. That lesson, based on Evans' faith, was that the best road to travel was the one that was straight and narrow, and the best way to pass the time was with an optimistic outlook.

Though known for her quick smile and hearty laugh, Dale Evans did not have an easy life. Long before she was famous, she was an unmarried teen mother. Even after she found success, she knew the pain of having children die. Thus the trails she rode were filled with deep valleys and rough weather. Yet rather than pity herself, she moved forward and found ways to help others through the same kind of tragedies she had experienced.

Christ was a lifter. He found people who had been rejected by society, had few friends and no hope, and assured them they were loved and their lives had meaning. Even before they realized He was the Son

of God, just through His actions, Jesus inspired others to follow His lead.

Each of us has trials, and as Dale Evans wrote it "Happy Trails," it is how we deal with them that defines our faith. We will see many on the trails of life, and if we follow in the footsteps of Christ, then we will do our best to assure each of those we meet they have value. In doing this simple act, we bring a bit of happiness into the world and become a lifter of spirits just like Jesus.

$\mathscr{H}$e's Got the Whole World in His Hands

We know that God works all things together for good for the ones who love God, for those who are called according to his purpose. —Romans 8:28

In the late 1950s, life for many was a scary proposition. The Cold War had escalated to a point where duck-and-cover drills were practiced on a regular basis in schools. Thousands of preachers were also using the nuclear age as a signal for the end of the world. Many people believed a war between the United States and Soviet Union would soon bring about the destruction of mankind. A newspaper editorial of the day signaled the attitudes of millions when it announced, "God Is Dead." And with the power to destroy billions resting in the hands of just a few people, it at least seemed like God had stepped back and become a spectator.

In the midst of all this hopelessness, a child's voice reassured the world that God was still in charge.

Laurie London, a young British boy, stepped into the recording studio and cut an American song that was likely a century and a half old. When released, millions seized "He's God the Whole World in His Hands" as if it were life preserver thrown to a drowning shipwreck victim. Audiences the world over simply couldn't get enough of the affirmation that God was out there and caring about them.

"He's Got the Whole World in His Hands" was born in the fields of the American south. It was written by a slave whose name we will never know. That man or woman likely experienced more trouble and suffering than any person in the modern age. He or she was not considered human by a society that viewed bondage as a necessary evil. So the writer of this hymn was not in charge of the present and had no control over the future. His or her owner could beat him or her to death, and there would be no punishment. He or she could be sold on an auction block on a minute's notice. Yet in the face of a life with no promise of freedom, this slave found solace in faith. Somehow this Christian still believed that a loving God was in charge.

There is strange irony in having the words of slave, a man or woman who truly was the least of these, remind the free people living in the most powerful country in the world that God is in charge. Yet when "He's Got the Whole World in His Hands" was released, that was just what happened. Many turned back to the Bible to search for hope, and they found it. A child's voice and a slave's anthem were the wake-up call for millions of insecure Christians.

The world survived the Cold War. The destruction that millions predicted did not happen. In retrospect, it seemed that God was in control, and those who didn't succumb to panic and instead relied on faith were right. Today there are still millions looking at every bump in the road as proof the world is about to end. They live in such fear they fail enjoy the wonderful moments they have been given. If a slave can see that God is alive and has a great plan for each life and if a slave can be secure in faith, then surely we can be too.

DOWN BY THE RIVERSIDE

All have sinned and fall short of God's glory, but all are treated
as righteous freely by his grace because of a ransom that was
paid by Christ Jesus. —Romans 3:23-24

"Down by the Riverside" is one of the more upbeat of the spirituals. Even though the slave who wrote the song cannot be identified, it is easy to spotlight the group that brought this rousing number to national attention. The Fisk University Jubilee Quartet produced a hit record of "Down by the Riverside" in 1920. By the time World War II began, the century-old song had been cut more than a dozen other times and had become one of the country's most popular choral anthems.

"Down by the Riverside" has several unique themes woven into a narrative about crossing Jordan and entering heaven. So while most see the song as pointing to the rewards of the hereafter, this spiritual also subtly presents some truth about life on earth and the freeing power of prayer.

With lyrics that focus on laying down the weapons of war, "Down by the Riverside" initially appears to be an antiwar ballad. This is a unique view for a song written by a slave who was not allowed to fight in war. Most spirituals centered on heaven as a place where the burdens of a life of bondage would end. Several scholars have therefore wondered if the song's lyrics had not one but two meanings. The obvious is the rewards of faith with a life spent without worry in heaven. The second centers on the burdens that can be eased through prayer.

A friend of mine once asked me who was the most important person in my life beyond my family. I tried several different answers—all wrong—before finally giving up. My friend then told me my optimistic attitude would not last very long if the garbage man quit coming to my house each week. When the trash starting piling up, insects and rodents would invade my world. Soon thereafter would come sickness. She assured me that without the good work of the garbage man, I would quickly become a pessimist.

When we accept Christ as our Savior, the rewards are far greater than just a pass through heaven's gate. Beyond having our sins forgiven, we have the chance to pray and give Jesus our troubles. Our conversations with the Lord enable us to put voice to our worries. And it is in prayer that we have the chance to have God take our problems, leaving us with a clear mind and a new vision. Without prayer, all the trash we have been collecting in our heads stays there and corrupts our lives while negatively impacting our faith.

Today is a good day to lay down your burdens and celebrate your freedom from worry. Christ is ready to take that load and let you deal with the things that matter most in your life. It all begins with that honest dialogue we call prayer.

Swing Low, Sweet Chariot

Then you will know the truth, and the truth will set you free.
—*John 8:32*

"Swing Low, Sweet Chariot" is one of the few spirituals that can be traced back to the composer. Wallis Willis was a freed slave of mixed race who wandered west and ended up in the Indian Territory on a reservation near what is now Hugo, Oklahoma. The part Choctaw freedman would tell those who heard him sing his own gospel song that it had been inspired by 2 Kings 2:11: "They were walking along, talking, when suddenly a fiery chariot and fiery horses appeared and separated the two of them. Then Elijah went to heaven in a windstorm." Willis' slow moving ballad embraced the chariot as the vehicle that transported a man's soul to heaven. The inspiration to add the River Jordan to the mix came when the writer viewed the Red River separating the territory from Texas.

The song would have likely never been known beyond Oklahoma if Alexander Reid had not been teaching at Old Spencer Academy and heard Willis sing "Swing Low, Sweet Chariot" during an assembly. Reid recorded the lyrics and melody and sent them to Nashville, Tennessee. The famed Fisk Jubilee Singers picked up the gospel number and performed it on a national tour. It was soon published, distributed worldwide, and quickly became the best known spiritual.

"Swing Low, Sweet Chariot" embraces the tone of a weary traveler slowly making his way toward a final destination. In a real sense, it is autobiographical hitting the high points of a life that has been filled with both good times and bad. The defining moment of this life well lived is when the singer accepts Christ.

There is an old saying that goes, "If you don't know where you're going you will never know when you arrive." That is a reality for many people. They wander through life with no plan or road map. Without faith as a stabilizing factor, they often find life's journey frustrating and unrewarding. With no plan of their own, they tend to hitch rides with others, allowing them to control the direction of their decisions. In a very real sense, they are slaves to the world.

For a Christian, the destination is set, but to avoid the pitfalls of a sinful life, we still must keep our eyes on our course. Believing might get us a ride on the chariot, but the depth of our commitment can only be seen in the way we move toward heaven. If we fail to keep God's commandments, if we do not seek out places for service, if we don't try to live a moral life and treat others with compassion and love, then we are not taking the gift Jesus gave us seriously. While that might not cost us a trip to an eternal reward, it could lead others far enough astray so that they never get the ticket for that final ride.

Wallis Willis composed one other classic gospel song. In his "Steal Away and Pray," he wrote of a life centered by both prayer and study. In his words, Willis proves he not only wanted to die a Christian but also wanted to live as a Christian too. That should be the goal we all seek and embrace. When we do that, we will be set completely free from the bonds of this world an experience the ride of a lifetime.

O Happy Day

Or don't you know that all who were baptized into Christ Jesus were baptized into his death? Therefore, we were buried together with him through baptism into his death, so that just as Christ was raised from the dead through the glory of the Father, we too can walk in newness of life. —Romans 6:3-4

Philip Doddridge was one of twenty children born to a London couple. He and one sibling were the only two to reach adulthood. Eighteen other children died from disease, neglect, and violence brought on by poverty. Pulled off the streets by a school teacher, cleaned up and educated, the young man would accept Jesus as his Savior as a teen and surrender to preach in 1729 at the age of twenty-seven.

Doddridge, who had experienced such a sad, depressing childhood, was an upbeat, outgoing, cheery adult. When asked about his happiness, he always pointed to the "Happy day that fixed my choice." He would explain that was when he found hope, love, and compassion. No one realized until his death that Doddridge had written a poem about his salvation experience. When "O Happy Day" was discovered among his effects, it was set to an established melody and published. When the song arrived in the United States shortly before the revolution, a chorus was written to go with the original verses, and Edward R. Rimbault added new music.

"O Happy Day" was a standard in hymnals for more than a century, but in time, the song was largely forgotten. Doddridge's old hymn might have been lost forever if Edwin Hawkins hadn't formed a teen choir in Oakland, California. Hawkins's purpose for bringing the kids together was twofold. The first was to teach them gospel music, and the second was to pull them off troubled streets and feed their souls. Thus many of the kids in this choir were offered a second chance exactly like the one that saved Philip Doddridge two-and-a-half centuries before. In 1969, with Paul Anka producing the session, the Edwin Hawkins Singers cut "O Happy Day," and the hymn became a chart-topping hit.

"O Happy Day" is the story of one man's salvation experience. The short, simple lyrics put the spotlight on the emotions of the moment when Philip Doddridge accepted Christ. Yet the great lesson taught in

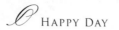

the song concerns more than just a moment. Dod-dridge, whose life had been so difficult, wasn't just happy when he found Jesus; he stayed that way for the rest of his life. Salvation didn't just save him, it changed everything including his mood.

Too many Christians don't embrace the joy of knowing they are saved. They don't celebrate a life where the destination is fixed. Yet if Christ is in our hearts, then how can we be dour? "O Happy Day" as sung by the Edwin Hawkins Singers fully captured the spirit of Philip Doddridge's testimony and fully presented the emotion every Christian should claim. The enthusiasm and joy offered through salvation is not momentary but life altering. You have a lot to celebrate, and it is time to begin. Today should be the starting point for an endless line of happy days!

$\mathscr{A}$MEN

If you have faith, you will receive whatever you pray for.
—*Matthew 21:22*

In 1963, Sidney Poitier starred in the hit film *Lilies of the Field*. For the movie, Jester Hairston wrote an original song that was inspired by the feel and message of spirituals. It was appropriate choice as Poitier's character was working for a group of nuns, and their relationship had grown to the point where each party shared a bit of their culture and faith with the other. "Amen" was thus the perfect song for Poitier to teach the nuns.

Amen is one of the most used words in daily Christian life. We end prayers with it, we show agreement with a line in a sermon by saying it, and we even shout it after hearing a rousing musical special. Yet most have no idea what amen really means or why it is used in so many different ways.

When we end a prayer with "amen," it means, "So be it." When we "amen" at a point in a speech or a sermon we are saying, "truly." When we cry out "amen" after a moving musical moment, we are essentially adding a "wonderful" to the "truly."

When it comes to prayer, "amen" is the final word. For many, knowing that *amen* means "so be it" takes prayer to another level. If you are asking for health and you end it with an "amen," then your request is made far more personal when you say, "so be it." It cements the fact that you believe God will make it happen. That makes a simple *amen* pretty powerful stuff. But it also puts a spotlight on what we really should be asking of God.

One of the first things we should recognize in Christ is His unselfishness. How many times in Scripture can you find Jesus asking for something? If we have Christ in our hearts, then we should reflect Him even in the way we pray. If we think like Jesus, then we automatically know that prayers are not meant to be selfish. We are to ask for things we need, not things we want. We are to turn to God to help us with things we can't do on our own not to give us the answers that are easily found. For us to honestly say, "so be it" after our prayer, we need to actually want "His will to be done" much more than we want our will to be satisfied.

The Lord's Prayer is a classic example of how we

should pray. Jesus didn't ask for wealth; instead He taught us to ask for what would sustain us today. Then Christ said we should forgive those who have wronged us and ask forgiveness for the ways we have sinned against God and against man. Then He told us we should ask God to help us make good choices and avoid bad ones. As we pray, we must become so Christlike in our pleas that we can actually mean that final "amen."

So be it! Those three words carry such a powerful punch that the words that precede them should always be carefully chosen. Amen.

WILL THE CIRCLE BE UNBROKEN

Jesus replied, "I assure you that today you will be with me in paradise." —Luke 23:43

"Will the Circle Be Unbroken" was written by noted hymn composer Charles Gabriel and his partner Ada Habersoln. It had been popular in southern churches for at least a generation when country music star A. P. Carter reworked it in 1935. Revamping the lyrics and slightly changing the title to "Can the Circle Be Unbroken," Carter brought his famed Carter Family into the studio and cut the number. His motivation was simple; his wife had recently divorced him, and he wanted to find a way to bring her back. Sadly, though the song was a hit, the couple never reconciled.

Johnny Cash would give the Carter Family hit new life thirty years later as a part of his composition "Daddy Sang Bass." Then the Nitty Gritty Dirt Band brought the greatest names in country music into a recording studio to cut the old standard.

The question asked in "Will the Circle Be Unbroken" is a haunting one. The answer requires having enough faith to believe that Jesus meant what He said in Luke 23. He promised that all who believed in Him would have a life beyond earth. In making the promise, He assured us that even if earthly relationships might come and go, our bond with Jesus would remain solid forever.

With the faith that our relationship with the Lord is eternal, perhaps it is time to consider the state of our earthly relationships. How do we stand with our family and our friends? Is there a petty issue keeping us from someone we love? Is there something we can do to fix that problem?

It has been written that the two most difficult words to say are "I'm sorry." The next three most challenging words to verbalize are "I forgive you." In most cases, even if those words are pushed from our lips, they are followed by a much longer sentence that begins with "but." It is that latter qualifying word that makes "I'm sorry" and "I forgive you" moot. There is no real apology or forgiveness if we limit it by further explanation. Jesus didn't forgive us and then add "but I want you to know that I told you so" or "this wouldn't have happened if you had listened to me." And neither should we.

If we truly want to repair relationships, then we must be willing to love and forgive unconditionally. That means laying judgment to one side and taking the first step forward. Love is not about coming up to a set of predetermined standards. If that were the case, then Jesus wouldn't have shown love to the woman at the well or anyone else. None who have lived have come close to the standards set by Christ. Rather than picking up stones and tossing them or stubbornly waiting for a friend or loved one to approach us, we must make the first step. That is what Jesus would do and did do countless times. If a circle in your life is broken, then maybe it is time to see if simply saying, "I'm sorry," "I forgive you," or "I love you" will fix it. Even if it doesn't, it is still a good start.

LET IT BE ME

Then I heard the Lord's voice saying, "Whom should I send, and who will go for us?" I said, "I'm here; send me."
—Isaiah 6:8

One of the most commonly used of our long list of folk sayings is "He who hesitates is lost." There are many people who have been given credit for this old axiom, but trying to pin down the original source is difficult. I have a feeling that Moses might have even thought something similar when the children of Israel were wandering in the wilderness. Where the proverb came from is not nearly as important as the truth it points out. Waiting has consequences in almost everything from sports to love. For many, waiting for just the perfect moment or situation turns into a life filled with inaction and regret.

"Let It Be Me" was a French song written by Gilbert Becaud and Pierre Delanoe in 1955. Mann Curtis added the English lyrics two years later. The song did not become a hit until 1960 when the Everly

Brothers took it up rock and pop music charts all over the world.

"Let It Be Me" is really a plea for love. In its lyrics, the singer assures the one he loves he will always be there for her if she will just give him the chance. While the song spells out the singer's devotion, it also clearly shows that love is a two-way street. The song leaves us hanging as we never find out if the singer's love is accepted.

We have confidence Christ accepts and loves us. We don't have to wait and hope that we will somehow appeal to Him. Jesus welcomes us in spite of our faults. So for Christians, "let it be me" has a much different connotation than it does for someone seeking love. For us, "let it be" should not be about waiting but about action.

We are taught that we must strive to become more like Christ. We must emulate Jesus in our words and life. We should jump at the opportunities we have to do this. But most Christians have the habit of hesitating when offered the chance to put their faith into action.

When we think of our role as Christians, we should not hesitate to say, "Let me be the one to carry the cross, let me carry others' burdens, and let me be the one to talk to you about my faith." While we won't lose our salvation if don't show this kind of enthusiasm, someone else might never gain his or hers. In Isaiah, the writer states very clearly, "I am here so you can send me." That needs to be our motto today!

Jumping at the chance to serve God doesn't usually mean you will be sent to a remote part of the world. There are opportunities everywhere in your neighborhood, church, or school. Don't hesitate to call a sick friend, be there for someone who is grieving, or take on a role at church. The thing to always remember is that God is calling you just as clearly as He is the missionary. To hear Him, just listen and then respond by saying, "Let it be me."

$\mathscr{H}$OW GREAT THOU ART

In the midst of America's darkest days, Franklin Roosevelt said, "The only thing we have to fear is fear itself." Fear has a paralyzing affect on people. It can dig in so deeply into minds that even Christians often forget there is a much greater force watching out for them.

While they were sailing, he fell asleep. Gale-force winds swept down on the lake. The boat was filling up with water and they were in danger. So they went and woke Jesus, shouting, "Master, Master, we're going to drown!" But he got up and gave orders to the wind and the violent waves. The storm died down and it was calm. He said to his disciples, "Where is your faith?" Filled with awe and wonder, they said to each other, "Who is this? He commands even the winds and the water, and they obey him!" —Luke 8:23-25.

On an 1880s summer day, a young Swedish preacher was suddenly caught in a violent thunderstorm. From the safety of a barn, he watched in fearful awe as torrents of rain poured down. Then as quickly as it appeared, the storm dissipated and Carl Boberg stepped back into a world fresh and alive. The fear that had gripped him for a few minutes turned to joy and exhilaration in having so closely witnessed God's magnificence and power. A few days later, Boberg recorded his memories of that experience in a poem he shared with his congregation. Those verses, later coupled with an old folk melody, are now known as "How Great Thou Art."

If you have read the New Testament's accounts of Christ's life, then you know that Boberg was not the first to find himself deeply frightened by a storm. It was on a sailing trip that the disciples were brought to their knees by powerful wind, rain, and waves. With their boat filling with water, they woke up Jesus and shared their fears. Christ asked them a simple question, "Where is your faith?" He also commanded the storm to cease. It was at this moment the twelve men who had been following Jesus began to understand this was more than just a charismatic leader.

The storms of life are many. They come in a wide variety of forms. They rain down on the just and unjust. They play no favorites. It is how we deal with the storm that defines the depth of our faith. Do we fall apart or do we embrace the knowledge that God is with us even when the skies are dark and the lightning is flashing?

My grandmother used to say, "You have to have the rainy days to fully appreciate the sunshine." In spite of the fact she was a poor woman who saw two of her ten children die, Grandma found the faith to push forward. She didn't worry about the storms but instead saw in them God's incredible power. She never talked about what she didn't have but rather about how thankful she was for what she did have. She didn't lament what she had lost but rather expressed joy about what she had gained. The next time a storm visits you, start dealing with it by counting your blessings. After all, we have nothing to fear, not even fear itself, if we have faith.

$\mathcal{T}$O DREAM
THE IMPOSSIBLE DREAM

Jesus looked at them carefully and said, "It's impossible for human beings. But all things are possible for God."
—*Matthew 19:26*

For generations it has been said that, in America, any person can grow up and be the president. Yet for all the optimism attached to this image, many more people have taken the attitude that dreaming about beating the odds and having great success is a waste of time. There are those who even preach that people should just be satisfied with their lots in life and not try to exceed them because that will just set them up for heartache.

In the 1965 award-winning musical *Man of La Mancha*, Mitch Leigh and Joe Darion composed a song for the eternally optimistic Don Quixote. "To Dream the Impossible Dream" is the musical theme in this play about following a quest. As successful as this Tony-winning play was, the musical's most popular song took on a life of its own. For millions, "To Dream the Impossible Dream" became their theme song as they sought to achieve goals that most felt were well beyond their means and abilities.

It has been written that while there might be deep heartbreak in losing, there is even greater shame in not trying. Those who achieve their dreams are like Don Quixote; they have the ability to fail and bounce back. They don't allow the missteps or perceptions of others to keep them from trying again and again. They dream big because they sense that the impossible can happen.

The same thing has happened to me and to many others who knew we had something special but couldn't get anyone to listen. One of my bestselling books was rejected twenty-seven times. Andy Andrews's first best-seller, *The Traveler's Gift* was rejected seventeen times and only published because the publisher's wife read the manuscript and insisted that he look at it again. Every major Christian publishing house in America turned down the Left Behind series except one, but that one, Tyndale House, made it the number-one best-selling Christian fiction series in history.

Why did each of us keep plugging away when year after year we were told no? Why didn't we give up when the top people in the industry told us our ideas had no merit? The answer is partially found in the optimism of "To Dream the Impossible Dream," but there was something else added to the mix. That was the promise found in Matthew 19:26. In each case, we each had the faith that God was with us on our quest.

The disciples were scared to follow Jesus as He walked on water. As they considered the challenge, their logic overrode their faith. Yet the key to doing the impossible was to trust and not look down. You likely have a dream, and no matter your age, with enough faith, you can still try to make it a reality. There are no guarantees of success, but the quest will be worth the effort and will likely inspire others to seek their dreams. Take a step of faith and don't look back. After all, Jesus assured us the impossible is possible.

Happy Birthday to You

I know that there's nothing better for them but to enjoy them-selves and do what's good while they live. Moreover, this is the gift of God: that all people should eat, drink, and enjoy the results of their hard work. —Ecclesiastes 3:12-13

There are several annual celebrations that Americans embrace. These include Christmas, Valentine's Day, Easter, Mother's Day, Memorial Day, Father's Day, Independence Day, Labor Day, Veterans Day, and Thanksgiving. There are a few other holidays that get a passing nod, but they do not generate the sense of enthusiasm that is a part of these special ten. The activities associated with these days are corporate. The whole nation stops and acknowledges each one, therefore, it is America that comes together as a family on these special times. Yet there is one unique day that almost all of us celebrate that is not an official holiday. It is as individual as we are and yet likely as important to children as any day of the year.

"Happy Birthday to You" is one of the five best-known songs in the world. It started life as "Good Morning to All" and was sung in thousands of schools for generations. Sisters Patty and Mildred Hill penned "Good Morning to All" in 1893. They were teachers and wrote the song as part of an effort to come up with new methods of instructing elementary students. Using the same tune, "Happy Birthday to You" came along a generation later. It stayed in the public domain until the Great Depression when Preston Ware Orem and Mrs. R. R. Forman took credit for writing the words. Ironically, in recent times, the song is most famous for litigation based on the length of the copyright and fees issued for performance. Thus, for legal reasons, it is not sung in public nearly as much as it was a generation ago.

A fact of life seems to be that once most folks pass a certain age, their attitudes on birthdays change. Many no longer see them as times of celebration but as a realization that they are getting further and further away from the carefree days of youth. I know people who avoid birthdays altogether. Others I know will not even admit to their real age. For them, birthdays are anything but happy.

Those ignoring the passing of the years need to realize that birthdays are one of life's greatest blessings. If you dread getting another year older, stop and think about the folks you knew who didn't have the chance to have as many birthdays as you have had. Illness or accidents took them from their loved ones far too soon. While you may get many gifts on the anniversary of your birth, none are as precious as the fact God has given you another year to make an impact for Him. So after you hear the strains of "Happy Birthday to You," it might well be time to say a prayer of thanks for another year of life. In fact, when you think about the blessings of living, it might just be worth celebrating each day God gives us as a new and wonderful birthday. If you treat growing older as a gift, then it might just change your whole outlook on life!

ZIP-A-DEE-DOO-DAH

May the God of hope fill you with all joy and peace in faith so that you overflow with hope by the power of the Holy Spirit.
—Romans 15:13

Even when everything is going just the way you want, how many times do you stop, grin, and shout, "What a wonderful day?" In 1946, just months after a world war had ended, the songwriting team of Allie Wrubel and Ray Gilbert were embraced in a sense of wonderment as they sat down to compose a song for the Disney movie *Song of the South*. Using every symbol they could find for good fortune and joy, the pair created "Zip-A-Dee-Doo-Dah." The number fit so well with the Disney image that the company took it far beyond the film. It became a brand. When Disney built Disneyland, they hoped that each visitor would have a "Zip-A-Dee-Doo-Dah" experience.

To really experience life's "Zip-A-Dee-Doo-Dah" moments, we need to be able to see beyond what is

temporal and look at the wonders of creation. To do that we must either get rid of or control a few things that often block us from this experience. The first is worry.

We often become so worried about what might happen that we don't celebrate the good things that are already a part of our lives. I recently read the story of a woman who became so concerned that she was going to get cancer that she saw every ache and pain as the disease ravaging her body. She was only in her thirties when she wasted away and died. An autopsy found nothing wrong. The only thing to which doctors could point as a cause of death was worry.

Another issue that causes many to miss the happiest moments in life comes from not pausing long enough to actually notice them. For many folks, their to-do list is far more important than their have-done list. Thus when they accomplish something, they rush to the next task rather than pausing and celebrating what just happened. Their lives become nothing more than a blur. They could have had many "Zip-A-Dee-Doo-Dah" moments but put them all off until the time they had everything done. When they reached that goal, life was over.

Maybe the most important key to having those

"Zip-A-Dee-Doo-Dah" moments is to embrace the peace Jesus offers to us through faith. Peace brings satisfaction. Rather than being constantly driven to accomplish more and have more, peace creates a world where we stop and take inventory of what we already have. This taking stock of blessings can fill us with wonder and joy. It can bring on a childlike quality that pushes us to jump, skip, and even laugh.

Turn! Turn! Turn!

There's a season for everything and a time for every matter under the heavens: a time for giving birth and a time for dying, a time for planting and a time for uprooting what was planted, a time for killing and a time for healing, a time for tearing down and a time for building up, a time for crying and a time for laughing, a time for mourning and a time for dancing, a time for throwing stones and a time for gathering stones, a time for embracing and a time for avoiding embraces, a time for searching and a time for losing, a time for keeping and a time for throwing away, a time for tearing and a time for repairing, a time for keeping silent and a time for speaking, a time for loving and a time for hating, a time for war and a time for peace.
—*Ecclesiastes 3:1-8*

If you are ever asked to name the #1 rock single that claims the oldest lyrics, the clear choice is the Byrds' "Turn! Turn! Turn!" Released in 1965, the song was adapted by folk legend Pete Seeger from the King James translation of the first eight verses in the third chapter of Ecclesiastes. So, in what has to be the most unique story behind a hit song, King Solomon, born around 1000 BC, penned a hit during the midst of the rock revolution.

Solomon presents in eight simple verses that people and their specific needs always remain the same. The words clearly define the cycle of life. They speak of the way things have been for hundreds of generations in the past and will be for hundreds of generations in the future.

One of the elements that many miss while reading the verses is the validity of each season being of equal importance. While the Bible relishes and embraces youth and all its energy, it treats old age and its wisdom with equal passion. As you study Scripture, you begin to realize that there are no peak periods in life. Each day is of equal value, and that means God sees us as important and vital in every season of life.

The Lord used a boy to bring down a giant and an old man to lead thousands out of bondage. God used women as well as men. He used the saint and the sinner. He limits no one who possesses faith. No matter what season of life you are in, there is a way the Lord can use you. Therefore your greatest day could well be right now, next week, or next year, but for it to happen, you must follow God's lead and get involved in doing His work.

Three thousand years ago, a man wrote his thoughts on paper. Could Solomon have guessed that millions in a world thousands of miles from his own would take his simple poem and make it a major hit during one of the most traumatic periods of American history? He likely never had that thought in mind. Yet God realized that there would be a time when the words would be needed, cherished, and embraced, but for that to happen, first a king had to have the faith to write them down. Today is a day for you to believe that something God's leading you to do will make an impact too. This is your season!

LEAN ON ME

There are persons for companionship, but then there are friends who are more loyal than family. —Proverbs 18:24

Forty years ago, Bill Withers was fooling around on a small piano when he kept coming up with a repeating series of chords. As he played them, the phrase "lean on me" came into his mind. With that simple beginning, the performer/songwriter created what *Rolling Stone* magazine has called one of the greatest songs of all time.

"Lean on Me" embraces a theme that was simple, direct, and true. People simply can't make it by themselves. They must have folks they can trust to help them in any situation, at any time, and for any reason. But that is just the beginning of what leaning on others really means.

To be like Christ, friends will walk that extra mile. They will be honest with us but not judge us when we don't follow their advice. They will pick us up even if we have been wrong. Therefore the

difference between a companion and a friend is huge!

There are two questions everyone should ask concerning real friendship. (1) Who can I depend upon when my world is falling apart? (2) Who will be there for me during my toughest times? This first question defines how much faith we have in our safety net of friends. Yet, the strength of that net is based on the second question we must contemplate, and it goes much deeper than our initial query as it speaks to the way others see us.

If we are selfish, then others will not make the call to ask us for help. They will figure that our affection is shallow, our focus is in the mirror, and we will be too busy to take time for them. To assure yourself a friend will be there when you need him or her, then you must have the heart of a servant and be there for him or her too. If people see Christ in your life, if they see you living your faith, if they see you put your prayers into action through service, if they sense and see your words are sincere, then they know you will be there for them, and conversely, they will likely always be there for you. Friendship is a team project with both parties willing to pay the same price.

In the hit song "Lean on Me," the title is a promise that demands a great deal more than just a phone call now and then. It also puts each of us in a position of not fully being in control of our lives. If we are to be leaned on, then we will have to give up precious moments. It means we will lose sleep, have to sometimes rearrange our schedule, have to stop and help someone when we have other pressing needs on our schedule, and give up things we really want to do. In other words, we have to be like Jesus. That is a lot of work and takes some sacrifice, but the good news is the people whom others lean on will never be alone. In their toughest trials, they will always have friends who rally to their side.

$\mathcal{T}$OP OF THE WORLD

*"God is indeed my salvation; I will trust and won't be afraid.
Yah, the Lord, is my strength and my shield; he has become my
salvation." —Isaiah 12:2-3*

Sometimes even the experts miss something
very obvious. When song scribe John Bettis
teamed with Richard Carpenter to write new
music for the Carpenters, the pair created a number that was much different than what the group
had been recording. It was more country than rock
and was far more upbeat than the ballads of lost
love that had given the act several hits. But as the
Carpenters had just scored success saluting old
rock and roll in "Yesterday Once More," they
opted to include "Top of the World" on their
album "A Song For You." Buried with a dozen
other cuts, the Bettis/Carpenter composition
would have likely been lost to the world if country
singer Lynn Anderson hadn't bought the album.
Anderson heard something special in "Top of the

World," cut it, and took it to the top of the country charts in June 1973. Realizing they had overlooked the value and potential of one of their own songs, Richard and Karen returned to the studio, recorded a new version, and released "Top of the World" as a single in the fall of 1973. It would become one of the Carpenters' biggest hits.

The theme of "Top of the World" embraces the power of love. It promotes the belief that true love has the ability to make everything seem wonderful. The lyrics also proclaim that being in love is like being reborn into a new creation.

Many have compared "Top of the World" to the famous hymn "Love Lifted Me." Both compositions trumpet the power of love and its ability to change a person's perspective; the difference is that the Carpenters sang of the love between a man and a woman whereas the old hymn embraced something much deeper.

God's love is something that should constantly lift us above the struggling masses. When we accepted Him, we become a part of a new creation. The fears that filled our lives have been replaced by faith. Rather than sinking in sin, we were lifted to a place where we are secure in the knowledge we are unconditionally accepted and loved. That feeling should stay with us forever. Yet for many, this spiritual high fades almost as quickly as it appears.

Any counselor will tell you that communication is the key to sustaining a marriage. This includes more than just talking; it means spending time with our spouses to rekindle the moments when we realized we were in love.

Christians also need to rekindle the fire. This is also done by communication. So we must pray. But we also need to read Scripture, listen to God's music, join in worship, and stay in touch with those who remind us that His love is forever. The best place to be lifted is usually found where most first discovered Jesus' love, and that is in church.

ℒet There Be Peace on Earth

Happy are people who make peace, because they will be called God's children. —Matthew 5:9

God gives us endless opportunities to restart our lives. He never gives up on us. But there are times when we have the power to blot out those endless opportunities for second chances. In the closing days of World War II, Jill Jackson was so overwhelmed by her problems that she was at the breaking point. Her husband had deserted her, she was unable to even scrape up the money to feed her little girl, she had no career options, and she was living in a place where she knew no one. With a background as an orphaned and abused child, Jill saw no hope. So she attempted suicide. But just like she had failed at seemingly everything, she didn't die. Now partially paralyzed, her life had even less promise than it had before. It would take years of searching for hope before she read Christ's story and suddenly felt a sense of peace she had never known. In Jesus, she finally discovered someone who would not reject her.

With faith in her heart and a new outlook on life, Jill met and fell in love with composer Sy Miller. Together the two began to write and, inspired by Jill's tragic story, they penned "Let There Be Peace on Earth." It would be almost a decade before they found a home for their song, but during the Vietnam War when people finally heard "Let There Be Peace on Earth," it became one of the era's most popular choral anthems. It then crossed over to Christmas music where it was transformed into a cherished carol.

Jill Jackson couldn't imagine any kind of peace until she found Christ. Crippled by her own hands, she nevertheless was spiritually healed when she accepted Jesus. The peace that flooded her soul sent her in a new direction where she found success as a woman, a mother, a wife, and a writer. It also led her to pen an anthem offering a formula for peace echoing back to the earliest days of the Christian church.

The first missionaries realized that Christianity is all about touching one soul and one life at a time. It was through this personal relationship that a movement began that today reaches billions. In places like

China, where the government has attempted to eliminate Christianity, the faith has grown, and there are more Christians in that country than in the United States. Those who have felt the peace brought by this faith were touched one-on-one by men and women who decided that sharing the gospel had to begin with them.

Jill came to the realization that things start to change when we begin the change. That led her to create a song that has inspired millions. Today you have a choice to either make a difference or to sit back and watch others do the heavy lifting. You can either take responsibility of letting the work of Christ start with you or leave it to another. Your faith will be defined by the choice you make as well your ability to bring peace to your own heart.

$\mathscr{I}$ Saw the Light

But you are a chosen race, a royal priesthood, a holy nation, a people who are God's own possession. You have become this people so that you may speak of the wonderful acts of the one who called you out of darkness into his amazing light. Once you weren't a people, but now you are God's people. Once you hadn't received mercy, but now you have received mercy.
—*1 Peter 2:9-10*

While others might have used the life of the Apostle Paul or evangelist Billy Sunday as a model for "I Saw the Light," country music legend Hank Williams only had to look in the mirror to find his inspiration. His reflection showed a wildly popular singer who millions adored, a genius when crafting lyrics and melodies, and a media icon as popular on radio and the new medium of television as he was on records. But the mirror also presented a man consumed by doubts, fears, and addiction. By 1950, the biggest post–World War II music star was a hopeless alcoholic. Yet even in the midst of his stupors, Hank managed to craft some of the most dynamic and moving songs in music history. One of them stands as a haunting reminder of the saddest aspects of his lonely life.

It is said that countless addicts have turned their lives around through the inspiration found in Hank's most famous gospel song. "I Saw the Light" spoke to them as clearly as the voice Paul heard when he was struck blind. So in a very real sense, Hank Williams has been responsible for leading many souls to faith. But as much as his words have opened that door out of the darkness for thousands, they couldn't help the singer find a way to free himself of his own doubts and addictions.

Just months before he died at the age of twenty-nine, Hank concluded another one of his sold-out concerts with "I Saw the Light." A few minutes later, as he rode with several other entertainers, he pulled a bottle out of his coat pocket and took a long draw. After swallowing the whiskey, he sadly observed, "That's the problem, there just ain't no light." As sad as that statement was, what was sadder was that on that night no one offered to help Hank.

You know where the light switches are in your home, but a visitor doesn't. If a friend were searching for a switch, would you allow him to search in the

darkness or would you turn it on for him? There are people all around us right now struggling in a dark world. They are consumed by hopelessness brought on by problems, depression, or addiction. Many see no way out. Will we offer them our help, compassion, and love, or will we just hope they manage to somehow find the switch? There is no question what Jesus would do.

"I Saw the Light" is both an inspired song and a sad testament to a hopeless life. Thus this song serves as reminder that many will not find the light by themselves. Those of us who know how to end the darkness will have to be the ones who show others where the light switch can found.

$\mathcal{S}$WEET, SWEET SPIRIT

*God caused the one who didn't know sin to be sin for our sake
so that through him we could become the righteousness of
God. —2 Corinthians 5:21*

More people were likely introduced to "Sweet, Sweet Spirit" while attending Elvis Presley concerts than ever heard it in a church service. In hundreds of shows, Presley stopped performing and asked a gospel quartet to sing that Doris Akers song. This unusual change of pace during a hard-driving performance put a bright spotlight on a song Presley deeply loved. During many shows, he actually begged the audience to listen to the lyrics and embrace what those words offered.

In 1962, Akers was the director of the Los Angeles Sky Pilot Choir. Each Sunday before church worship services, the choirmaster would demand her members join in deep prayer. She assured them that feeling the spirit in the heart was much more important to performance than their talent. Thanks to Akers intensity, it was not surprising these prayer sessions sometimes dragged on well past the time church services were scheduled to begin. One Sunday, when they were very late and the congregation was waiting, Akers noted a sweet spirit filling the room. This inspired the choir director to pen a song based on that experience.

The sweet spirit of God can enter you anywhere. It can come to you in a car or on a mountaintop. So there are likely times in each of our lives when it has come to us when we have been alone. But to most easily experience the power of God's spirit, it is usually necessary to be in a place where others are worshiping. When we are bound together in this environment, when we pool our resources, when we all get on the same page, great things seem to happen. The old timers would say, "God is working now." Thus it is important for each of us to find a church where we can join in prayer, song, and study. By doing so, we can more readily feel God's love and hear His calling.

God's spirit is everywhere and is always willing to enter our hearts. The question becomes, do we have the courage to allow it in? Giving that spirit entry means that we will begin to see the world as Christ did. Thus things that just a few minutes before seemed important will be lost in the light of grace.

The spirit will bring new priorities that will render some of our long-held material dreams moot and lead us in a direction where service takes precedence over the quest for earthly things. The sweet, sweet spirit is much more than a momentary high; it can represent a new outlook and drive. As it says in Akers' song, when we leave the place where we experienced the spirit, we will be changed forever.

$\mathscr{S}$TAND BY ME

Don't fear, because I am with you; don't be afraid, for I am your God. I will strengthen you, I will surely help you; I will hold you with my righteous strong hand. —Isaiah 41:10

Ben E. King's voice has been heard on scores of hits, first as the lead singer of the Drifters and later as a solo artist. The man was also a talented songwriter who drew some of his inspiration from African American church music. Charles Tindley, the former slave turned charismatic pastor and the father of black gospel music, wrote a song that King dearly loved, "(When the Storms of Life Are Raging) Stand by Me." This moving religious ballad provided the name and idea behind one of the rock and roll era's most recorded songs.

Though it was easy for King to begin his new version of the gospel classic, he struggled to finish "Stand by Me." Unable to come up with something he felt worthy of the concept, he went to the writing team of Jerry Leiber and Mike Stoller. Together the three men completed the song and worked up an arrangement. Yet even though he liked the final product, King initially passed on recording it. It would be much later that Leiber and Stoller finally convinced the singer to cut the trio's composition. That record quickly emerged as one of history's top hits and cemented King's status as a solo artist.

Charles Tindley wrote his "Stand by Me" to illustrate a sermon. He told the congregation that God's love was like a tree so heavily laden with fruit its branches all but dragged the ground. Therefore even the smallest child could easily pick an apple from that tree. Tindley then pointed out that this same tree was so strong it could withstand any storm. He closed by noting that each Christian should have deep roots, a strong trunk, and fruit that could and would be shared with any in need.

As Christians, we are supposed to stand by those in their moments of greatest trials. We are to provide them both spiritual and physical help. We are to do so without judgment and without expecting repayment. Thus we stand by them not as a job but as a calling. We minister to them because we want to be like Christ.

Tindley's sermon on the fruit tree is brilliant because is not just about sharing; it is also about

perception. What the tree is offering is visible and accessible. The question Tindley asked his congregation was to see what others saw in them. Did they hide their fruit? Did their attitudes push people away? Were they friendly, warm, and receptive? Did they smile easily and touch gently? Those who truly have the fruit of the spirit possess these qualities. And they also possess one more important gift. They are so strong in faith that others can sense they have the courage to weather the toughest storms of life. To be the one others want standing by them, you must work toward being like the fruit tree that inspired the original song.

E ARE FAMILY

But if we are children, we are also heirs. We are God's heirs and fellow heirs with Christ, if we really suffer with him so that we can also be glorified with him. —Romans 8:17

In 1979, Bernard Edwards and Nile Rodgers wrote an up-tempo song that seemed perfect for the disco era. They offered it to Atlantic Records who took a listen and sent the pair on their way. Undaunted the composers kept pitching until Atlantic gave "We Are Family" a second chance. Sister Sledge dropped it onto an album, and the label opted to try the song as a single. The infectious lyrics and easy-to-follow tune immediately caught the public's attention, and the record hit #1 in several different genres. Yet it probably would have died with disco if Willie Stargell and the Pittsburgh Pirates had not adopted it as the team's theme song. For years, night after night at Pirate home games, thousands joined their voices to declare they were all part of the same family.

The ballpark choir that sang "We Are Family"

ARE FAMILY

represented all races, classes, and faiths. They came
from different backgrounds and had far different life
experiences, but they were bonded by the love of base-
ball team. That song represented their feelings for each
other while they celebrated Pirate victories or mourned
defeats. No matter the final outcome and long after the
notes of their song had faded, when at the ballpark,
they continued to think of themselves as family.

Over the past two thousand years, the Christian
family has become a bit dysfunctional. Rather than
come together to celebrate our commonality as followers of Christ, many go their own way and treat
others as "lesser Christians." Rules have even been
created to reinforce this attitude. Denominations
often agree that most Christians are saved, but their
group does it the best way. This kind of thinking
splits the family of Christ into a wide variety of seg-
ments. Thus, the sense of brotherhood is lost because
the groups cannot find common goals and will not
work together.

I go to a church that spends a few weeks each year
rebuilding the homes of our city's poorest of the
poor. The church does not work on its own members'
homes but rather looks for those in the greatest need,
no matter their faith. This attitude has lead to several
different denominations joining us in this ministry.

Within a decade of beginning Arms Around Arkadelphia, more than one hundred homes have been rebuilt and countless men, women, and youth of various faiths have come together in this work. Much like the fans in Pittsburgh, when these Christians quit worrying about doctrine and concentrated on reaching "the least of these," they discovered that we are all a part of the same family.

Who are you willing to include in your family? Can you be as inclusive as the Pittsburgh fans? Can you forget race, status, and social standing in your Christian efforts? It is time we quit finding ways to separate ourselves and come together as a body of faith that shares a common Savior and a common goal. And this can start with each of us becoming as accepting as Christ was.

Unchained Melody

No one can serve two masters. Either you will hate the one and love the other, or you will be loyal to the one and have contempt for the other. You cannot serve God and wealth.
—Matthew 6:24

In 1955, Alex North and Hy Zaret were assigned to pen a title song for a low budget prison movie. Struggling to come up with an original point of view, they decided to put themselves into the role of prisoners. As they figuratively locked that iron door, a sense a darkness and loneliness took hold. Inspired by the realization of the hopelessness of being in love but being unable to see or hold the object of that love, they created a rare song whose title is never found in the lyrics. It is very likely that "Unchained Melody" would have been called "I Need Your Love" if it hadn't been used in the film *Unchained*.

The movie went almost unnoticed and was quickly forgotten though North and Zaret's song did find a place on charts when Jimmy Young scored a

#1 pop record with "Unchained Melody." Yet it would be a 1965 record sung by Bobby Hatfield of the Righteous Brothers that is now hailed as the definitive version of the ballad. Almost five decades later, Hatfield's cut of love and loneliness is still very much a part of America's musical landscape.

Those who find themselves in prison usually opted to ignore the spiritual in their quest for the material. Their lust to have what they wanted led them to take short cuts that circumvented the law. Thus the freedom they were seeking in pleasure and money was the trap that led them into bondage.

Though they might not end up behind bars, Christians who have strayed from God to chase physical satisfaction are enslaved as well. Though claiming every earthly thing that they thought they needed, they feel anything but free. Unhappy and directionless, a void in their soul cries out for a love that they just can't seem to find.

God's love does not restrict us; it frees us. It allows us to escape the pitfalls of temporary fixes and focus on the things that bring us real joy. Former American slave turned world-renowned educator Booker T. Washington defined the satisfaction found in Christian service with these words, "Those who are happiest are those who do the most for others."

"Unchained Melody" is a haunting song about love unrealized that contains an important moral lesson about the cost of seeking the material over the spiritual. Today is a good day to ask whom we serve and what goals in life we value. If we are struggling to claim happiness, if we are tempted to cut corners, if we are failing to serve others or even see those in great need, then it might be time to come up with some new priorities where faith determines our direction. Make that step, and freedom and happiness are just around the corner.